Going on Vocation

Texts for meditation about vocation

George Boronat

Scripture quotations are from The Revised Standard Version of the Bible: Catholic Edition, copyright © 1965, 1966 the Division of Christian Education of the National Council of the Churches of Christ in the United States of America. All rights reserved.

Copyright © 2019 by George Boronat. All rights reserved. This book or any portion thereof may not be reproduced or used in any manner whatsoever without the express written permission of the publisher except for the use of brief quotations. For permission requests, write to Contact-us in ipraywiththegospel.org

Rev. George Boronat M.D. S.T.D is a Catholic priest working in the Archdiocese of Southwark in London. He is the Chaplain of The Cedars School in Croydon, and of Kelston Club & Study Centre (Balham). He also works in Oakwood School (Purley) and has developed his pastoral ministry mainly with young people.

Index

Introduction 7
Foreword 13
1. Who are you? 17
2. God has a plan 21
3. Before the creation of the world 25
4. Go to Joseph 29
5. In order to be free, choose 33
6. Great expectations 37
7. Not me, not me 41
8. Trust 45
9. You have a vocation 49
10. Interior disposition 53
11. Blank cheque 57
12. Committing without knowing the consequences? 61
13. I can't do this! 65
14. Should I volunteer? 69
15. What if I simply can't say 'Yes'? 73
16. Getting ready 77
17. Prepare the soil 81
18. God wants the lot 85
19. God will change your plans 89
20. Resignation? 93
21. Simon of Cyrene 97
22. The freedom of the children of God 101
23. Let's put love and not duty at the centre 105
24. Mind your own business 109

25. Not all that glitters is gold 113
26. Prayer 119
27. God has put people there to help you 123
28. Do I have to do what I am told? 127
29. Trials 131
30. What if I say "No"? 135
31. This is not just about you 139
32. To fly high 143
33. Destroy the ships 147
34. You raise me up 151
35. To fill the gap 155
36. How can I be 100% sure? 159
37. The switch behind the door 163
38. Am I risking too much? 167
39. The prize 171
40. "Faithful in a very little, faithful also in much" 175
41. To be with Him 179
42. Just by chance? 183
43. Waiting for a signal 187
44. Saints were not saints inevitably 193
45. Expect opposition 199
46. In the thick of it 205
47. The Disciple Jesus Loved 211
48. Only one thing is necessary 217
49. Have you lost the star? Forwards! 221
50. Thank You! 227

"If you knew the gift of God," said Jesus to the Samaritan woman, "and who it is that is saying to you, 'Give me a drink'," (Jn 4:10). If you knew the gift of God...

If you knew how much He loves you,

If you knew how much He has suffered for you,

If you knew how much He expects from you,

If you knew how much He longs for your reply,

If you knew how many souls depend on it,

If you knew how much love the human heart can hold,

If you knew how much happiness the human soul can possess,

If only you knew Who is asking you to quench His thirst of love with yours...

If only you knew...

Introduction

> *He went up on the mountain, and called to him those whom he desired; and they came to him. And he appointed twelve, to be with him, and to be sent out to preach and have authority to cast out demons (Mk 3:13-15).*

"Vocation? Who...? Me? O, no, no... I want to get married, you know... to have kids and stuff..."

I was very amused by the reply of that 15-year-old boy when I asked him about his vocation. He was surprised at my reaction, but I couldn't help laughing out loud at the revelation that he was interested in having *"kids and stuff"*. One thing was clear: He didn't know what vocation meant.

Vocation, from the Latin, 'Vocare', means calling – and yes, even those who have *"kids and stuff"* have one. The misunderstanding is commonplace. For centuries the word was synonymous with religious vocation or vocation to Holy Orders. According to this mentality, those who have a vocation were called to become priests or friars, monks or nuns; and those who didn't have any of those callings just had *"kids and stuff"*, but no vocation. Thank goodness, the panorama changed and now it is universally accepted that even those who have *'kids and stuff'* have a vocation as well.

A fellow priest once asked my thoughts about the current *'vocation crisis'* in the Church. *"Why are we having fewer vocations?"* The Church has always had a vocation for each of her children, I clarified. The problem is that vocations have to be discovered, accepted, lived, fulfilled. As we read in the Gospel, Jesus *"called to him those whom he desired,"* but then they had to accept the call to follow Our Lord.

It may rather be a *'generosity crisis'* than a 'vocation' one. This affects every environment, every country, every institution. If there is a lack of commitment to marriage, who could be surprised that there is a lack of commitment to celibacy? If there is a lack of fidelity between spouses, who can be shocked at the lack of faithfulness in those called to consecrated lives?

Some may think that the problem is *'the people of the Church'* and by that, they understand mainly priests and monks and nuns. After twenty centuries some people still haven't grasped it. *'The people of the Church'* means every baptised person. However, they are right: the people of the Church are the problem.

You may be familiar with a popular story about an eagle-chick. During one of his hikes shepherding his flock, a farmer found an eagle's nest. He took an egg from the nest and placed it together with the other eggs that one of his chickens was sitting on; in time, the eagle-chick hatched together with the other younglings. Soon the eagle learned the customs of his adoptive siblings, walking through the yard, eating worms and corn and hopping about like the others. He even started daring to take longer jumps, to climb up a pole and crash to the ground, crying out with pride, just as other brave chickens did.

But on a certain day, the shadow of a bird soared through the skies. *"Who is that?"* he asked. A wise hen answered, *"It is an eagle that flies majestically, without any effort. But don't look at it anymore!*

Do not look at it, because our life is not like hers; our life is here, in the barnyard."

Some versions of the story tell about the farmer who, reflecting on the large wings of his majestic eagle, was surprised that it hadn't yet learned to fly. The bird had been cooped up his whole life. So, the farmer took the eagle in his arms to a nearby hill. There he pointed to the sky and said, "*You are an eagle. You belong to the heavens, not to the earth. Open your wings and fly!*" But the bird did not move. He looked down at the feeding chickens and hopped back to re-join them. The man tried again, "*Look at your wings, your beak, your size. You are no chicken! You shouldn't demean yourself by acting like those chickens. Spread out your wings and fly!*" But the young eagle only became more and more confused at this demanding challenge. By the look in his eyes, it was obvious that his only desire was to go back to his safe coop.

The farmer did not give up. He brought the eagle to a very high mountain. At the summit he lifted up the eagle once more and, extending his arms, he showed him the brilliant morning sun, saying encouragingly, "*You are an eagle. You were born to glide freely, to soar toward the sun. You can travel enormous distances and master the winds and currents. Don't be afraid. Open your wings and fly.*" The eagle, fascinated by the view from the heights of the summit, the colourful landscape under his talons, the abundance of light, and, especially, the presence of other majestic eagles soaring the clear skies, slowly opened his great wings.

And they took to the wind. With no more effort than that of stretching out his wings, his whole body started lifting up. He was scared and closed his wings quickly to crash back to the ground and grasp the rocks with his talons again. But something had changed. He now knew that he could fly. Once more he stretched out his wings to their full span, flapped them once and left the ground with a triumphant cry. He began to fly – higher and higher.

The story tells us that the eagle only looked back once. He flew past the farmer tracing an elegant circle and crying a majestic call as a way of thanking the man who made it possible for the eagle to *become* what he had always been.

The eagle could have had an easier life in the coop. After all, there was plenty of corn, lots of company and no stress. As an eagle among chickens, he would have had a very comfortable life since, being bigger than the average farm bird, he could choose the best corner of the barnyard and feast on the best worms.

Yes. He could have had an easier life, but not a happier one.

Going back to that shortage of vocations, could it not be that God *is sending* His Church eagles but they stubbornly prefer the commodities of the coop? Could it not be that there are too many eagles who have *chickened out*?

Could it not be that they never stopped to consider the span of their wings, their different colours and shapes and sizes? Could it not be that they just never thought they could be different from the rest of the poultry that surrounds them? Maybe they just don't know!

Some young eagles remain *chickens*, not because they want to stay in the yard, but because they never really wanted to fly away. They are with the rest of the chickens not because they said 'No' to becoming an eagle, but because they never said 'Yes' and the coop was the default position. There are people who don't follow their vocation, not because they say 'No' to God but because they never said 'Yes' to Him.

Some are afraid to fly, or most likely, to crash. But you may have seen birds learning to fly. They would spend their lives flapping their wings if they were not encouraged by their mothers – and even pushed sometimes – to take a leap. They can't learn to fly on the very first attempt and without any scratches. To soar the skies you need to take risks and trust the winds (the Holy Spirit).

In these pages you will find a book presented in short chapters to take to your prayer: a guide for young eagles to begin to soar the heights.

"Don't flutter about like a hen," wrote St Josemaría, *"when you can soar to the heights of an eagle."*

Holy Mary, Queen of the Apostles, Mother of Good Counsel, Seat of Wisdom, Handmaid of the Lord, may these pages help young souls, young eagles, to pray about their vocation; to converse with God about their calling and ask for the graces they need to get rid of their fears; to open wide their wings, catch the current of the Holy Spirit's winds, release their talons from the branches of the trees; to look up into the sun (the Son of God) and to fly, soar; to fall in love with the resplendent skies, the magnificent sights and the closeness of Heaven; to glide over the storms of this world and to never stop flying to the heights, higher and higher; to never give up, never again settle for a mediocre fluttering, until they find their rest in you, Mother, and in your Son, with the Father, in the Holy Spirit. Amen.

Foreword

Lines for those 'Farmers'

> *Barnabas went to Tarsus to look for Saul; and when he had found him, he brought him to Antioch. For a whole year they met with the church, and taught a large company of people* (*Acts* 11:25-26).

We celebrate the Apostle of the Gentiles with great devotion. St Paul has two feast days in the liturgical calendar, like St Joseph, St Peter and St John the Baptist. St Barnabas is not that well known and devotion to him is not so widespread. However, it was St Barnabas who made Saul the Apostle of the Gentiles. It was he who insistently pushed him to preach. St Barnabas was a relentless headhunter.

These few lines are suited to those souls who are in search of other souls. Those who have the mission of encouraging eagle-chicks to take the leap, to discover what they can do and to allow them to become what they are.

We were considering that 'vocation crisis' in the previous chapter. It also begs the question: could it be that *farmers* have given up, that they are not taking eagles to the heights, that they don't encourage them to open their wings, don't help them catch their first winds and urge them to fly?

Or could it be that eagle-chicks have no other eagles to inspire them? Could it be that they can't find majestic eagles they could look up to? Could it be that they can't see magnificent creatures gliding on the winds that could stir their desires to soar the skies themselves? Could it not be that they have lost sight of the saints: the St Johns, St Teresas, St Marys, St Ignatiuses, St Francises and Franceses, St Josephs, St Peters, St Pauls, St Augustines; and the plethora of holy eagles who have soared the skies before us and we have stopped looking up to?

Before we criticise the chicks, could we think of anything else we can do to help them fly?

The life of St Jean Marie Vianney is well known. On his path to ordination he met many difficulties. When he started glimpsing his vocation he was about 17. He had completed only one year of school education and was working full time with his father in the fields. His father wouldn't hear of his son becoming a priest and for two years the young lad was only sustained by the encouragement of his mother.

Finally his father gave in and his mother went to ask the parish priest to allow him to join in the classes he was giving to other children. Initially, the Abbé Charles Bailey thought the boy was too old. The other pupils were children of eleven and twelve and Jean Marie was already twenty. The priest agreed, however, to talk to him in person. If there are memorable moments in the history of every saint, this encounter was certainly Jean Marie's. The Abbé Bailey was ready to dismiss the boy until he met him in person: *"If it's this lad,"* he said, *"I'll take him on right away."*

Due to the difference in age and to his palpable difficulties in learning, Jean Marie became the mockery of his fellow pupils. The very same lessons they sailed through so easily had Jean Marie on the rack. After months of this he had made almost no progress. The young lad lost heart and communicated his intention to go back to the farm. But Mgr. Bailey knew his intentions and dissuaded him. He used an argument that he knew would target the very heart of the youth: if you go, he said, *"it's good-bye to all your dreams, Jean Marie; good-bye to the priesthood, good-bye to the care of souls."* The Abbé Bailey had hit the sensitive point and Jean Marie stayed.

But then, in 1809 he was drafted into the army. After some incidents, he became an "involuntary deserter" and had to hide for a while in a remote town. In 1811 he managed to get back to his parents' home. He was 25. He joined the seminary and his problems multiplied. Since his academic grades were not very promising, he took private tuition with some teachers to prepare for his exams. The problem was that he seemed to grasp the lessons, but as soon as he was questioned in Latin, he was lost. The results for Jean Marie Vianney were lamentable and in December 1813 he was asked to leave the seminary.

On his way home he tried to join the Lyons novitiate of the Brothers of the Christian Schools, but they asked him to think about it a bit more. When he told Abbé Bailey about his problems in the seminary, all the old priest said was, *"I want you to continue your studies,"* and resumed the lessons with his pupil. They prepared the exams together, now in French instead of in Latin.

He went back to the seminary to take the exams again at the age of 27. But again they were in Latin and the pupil failed. The very next day found Abbé Bailey knocking at the office door of Abbé Bochard, president of the examination board, at the archbishop's palace. *"The poor boy was simply tongue-tied in front of all you grand folk,"* Abbé Bailey said. *"Come to my place, I beg you, and bring the superior of the seminary with you, if you possibly can; then you'll see. We've absolutely got to keep a man like him in the diocese."*

The Abbé Bailey got his way. When he was examined at the presbytery Jean Marie *"answered the questions put to him very well."* And when Abbé Bochard consulted his colleague, Abbé Courbon, the latter, with whom rested the final responsibility for selecting candidates for ordination, simply asked, *"Is Monsieur Vianney devout? ... Has he a special veneration for Our Lady? ... Can he say his rosary?"*

"Yes, he's a model of devotion," he was told.

"Very well, I will take him. The grace of God will do the rest."

At the age of 29, on August 13, 1815, in the chapel of the seminary at Grenoble, he became a priest for all eternity. "If I were ever to become a priest," he had told his mother long before, "I should want to win many, many souls." Well, he did.

This story is not about Jean Marie; it's about Abbé Charles Bailey. How much the Church owes to this almost-unknown priest of the small village of Ecully who didn't give up and supported the seminarian *even when Jean Marie had himself given up!*

Behind every vocation there is an unwavering, persevering, enthusiastic *farmer* who was himself an eagle-chick once upon a time and knows the drill. Behind every vocation God has placed a person who believes in the possibilities of a newly-hatched eagle and will not give up until the chick can freely soar the skies.

Is there a crisis of vocations? May it not be a crisis of *farmers*?

Let us turn to Our Lady, the Mother of all Christians, to ask for the perseverance of those souls who search for other eagles to help them fly. Mary, Morning Star, we place under your intercession the souls of those who are in charge of bringing other souls, so that they never get discouraged when the eagle-chicks take their time, when they hesitate for too long, when they fly back to the coop looking for a more comfortable life. With your help, may those *farmers* never give up.

1

Who are you?

> *They asked John, "Who are you?" He confessed, he did not deny, but confessed, "I am not the Christ." And they asked him, "What then? Are you Eli'jah?" He said, "I am not." "Are you the prophet?" And he answered, "No." They said to him then, "Who are you? Let us have an answer for those who sent us. What do you say about yourself?" (Jn 1:19-22).*

You are asked this question on the phone, over the intercom, when you present an application, at border control or in an interview. *'Who are you?'* And we usually reply with a name: *'Brian Smith.'* That's the proper answer to the question, *'What's your name?'* But we are not just a name. Your name does not define you, it just identifies you. You can say *'That's a dog'*, *'That's an ice cream'*, *'That's a star.'* However, you would never say *'That's a Brian Smith.'* You are more than just a name. You are a child of God, a project of God, a person with a mission. In fact, to be precise, you are still 'under construction' like a building - or even better, a work of art that isn't yet finished. If an artist was asked about his work before he had finished, he would not say, *'This is a work of art'* or *'This is a landscape.'* He would say, *'I am painting a landscape,'* or *'It will be a nice landscape of the countryside but it's still in progress.'*

We are in the process of becoming what God planned us to be. We will discover in the end exactly who we are. If you had asked Karol Wojtyla who he was in 1930, when he was 10 years old, he would have told you that he was the son of Karol Wojtyla Snr. If you had asked him a few years later he would have told you that he was a seminarian. Later on he would have told you that he was the Bishop of Krakow and later still that he was Cardinal Wojtyla. But today he is not known as Karol Wojtyla, or as the son of his father or as a Bishop or Cardinal. He is St John Paul II. That's the answer to 'Who' he is.

You and I are a sketch of the saint we are to be. We are an *'unfinished project'*. In order to know exactly who we are, we need to trust the Architect and follow His instructions. God didn't ask young Karol Wojtyla to prepare himself to be Pope. God prepared him. What God asked of him was to become a priest. Once he had done what God wanted, God asked him to become a bishop. Until he had taken that step, he couldn't go to the next stage. God never discloses His entire plan in one go. And the same will happen with your vocation. When you sincerely decide to take your vocation to your prayer, you are starting to ask God for the next move.

If you don't make the move, then you will stay as an *unfinished project* all your life. It will be like the underground train system planned, but only half built, for Cincinnati in Ohio during the 1920s. It was a casualty of The Great Depression. Today you can visit the unused tunnels to witness what has been described as 'one of the city's biggest embarrassments'. It reminds us of Our Lord's parable about the man who started building but never finished and became the laughing stock of his neighbours because he *"began to build, and was not able to finish"* (Lk 14:28-30).

God made you for holiness, for happiness. And you only have one life, one shot. But if you do it right, one life is enough.

In 2009, nurse Bronnie Ware wrote an online article called 'Regrets of the Dying' about her time as a palliative carer. Working with dying people and developing close relationships with them during their last weeks resulted in raw, honest conversations about life and death, including what the patients wished they had done differently. Regret Number One was: *"I wish I'd had the courage to live a life true to myself, not the life others expected of me."*

"This was the most common regret of all," Bronnie explained. *"When people realise that their life is almost over and look back clearly on it, it is easy to see how many dreams have gone unfulfilled"*. The real dream we are born with is the ambition to become what we were meant to be, the one God thought about before the creation of the world.

Interestingly, the fifth regret on the list was, *"I wish that I had let myself be happier."* It is sad to realise at the end of your life that you could have been happier but never chose to be. You know it well: happiness is a choice. God made you for that total happiness. It is yours. You are entitled to it. But you need to decide to achieve it by becoming the person God made you to be.

Now is the moment when you need to decide whether you want to continue or whether you'd prefer to stop reading and start browsing through the sports news or wasting your time on YouTube. This is a serious invitation to be honest; honest with yourself and honest with God.

The story is told of a young girl who was praying about her vocation. She would go to church and spend time in front of a statue of Our Lady with the Child in her arms. She didn't know whether she should become a nun or find a man and get married: in her own words, whether to become a 'Sister' or a 'mother'. For weeks she repeated the same prayer, *"Holy Mary, shall I become a mother or a Sister?"* After insisting for a long time, one day the Child in the statue suddenly turned to the young woman and said, *"A Sister!"* She was shocked for an instant; but then reacted quickly and said, *"Be quiet! I am talking with your Mother..."*

If you start asking Our Lord for your vocation, make sure that you want to know God's Will - not out of curiosity, but out of a sincere resolution to follow the Architect's plans. If you think you want to follow God out of love for Him then tell Him now that you want to know His Will in order to fulfil it with His help. If you pray like that… do you doubt that Jesus will smile at you and assist you on this journey that you are beginning now?

Mary, Mother of Jesus and my Mother, please help me to give God the same answer that you gave when Gabriel revealed your vocation to you.

OK, Lord. I am ready. What do you want of me… now?

Through your intercession, Mary, my Mother, may I travel safely on this journey to discover God's Will for me; may the Lord walk with me, may St Joseph assist me and may my Guardian Angel keep me company along the way.

2

God has a plan

> *Blessed be the God and Father of our Lord Jesus Christ, who has blessed us in Christ with every spiritual blessing in the heavenly places, even as he chose us in him before the foundation of the world, that we should be holy and blameless before him. He destined us in love to be his sons through Jesus Christ, according to the purpose of his will* (Eph 1:3-5).

There is a song by the group '*Swedish House Mafia*' called "*Don't You Worry Child.*" The lyrics go like this: "*I still remember how it all changed; My father said, 'Don't you worry, don't you worry, child, see Heaven's got a plan for you; don't you worry, don't you worry now.'*" It all changed then, when the Father said to the child: don't worry, Heaven's got a plan for you. You were meant for something great. It should not worry you. It should fill you with hope. There are great things in store for you.

Bl John Henry Newman wrote: "*God has created me to do Him some definite service. He has committed some work to me which He has not committed to another. I have my mission. I may never know it in this life, but I shall be told it in the next. I am a link in a chain, a bond of connection between persons. He has not created me for naught. I shall do good; I shall do His work.*" It is a fact that God does not create people without a mission. When God thinks about someone, He thinks about what this person is meant to do in life. Everything in creation has a purpose. When God creates a bird He knows where it will fly, eat and die; and the bird gives glory to his Creator by flying, eating and dying. But He made us free, and therefore He is not expecting us to give glory to Him as a bird or a monkey, for they cannot love the Creator.

Jesus said many times to many different people, "*Come and follow me.*" But we never see those words followed by something like, '*and then, walking in single file, in a straight line, they started following Jesus.*' That would be weird. Imagine it: the Apostles walking in single file, like the Seven Dwarfs, all stopping at the same time and walking at the same pace, imitating Jesus like monkeys!

Some people may think of their vocation like that: a railway track. And once you decide to march on it you have less freedom to move than the wheels of a train. But vocation is not a train track. It is more of a mountain peak, a destination point – and you choose the way which suits you best to reach the summit; you choose the path, the rhythm, the pauses, the shoes... you do it *your way*, like Frank Sinatra. Because God made you *that way*.

How do we connect mission and freedom? An example might help. A great composer can have many things in mind when he composes a symphony. Well, God is *the* Great Composer. He knows all the members of the orchestra. He has given them their instruments, all perfectly tuned. He knows their abilities. He knows their rhythm. He is fully aware of their capacity because He designed them and their instruments *precisely* for that symphony.

Musicians are free, of course. They can follow their score or decide to play jazz. A violinist can envy the part played by another and decide to play that part as well, thinking that he can play it better. He probably can, but... will the symphony benefit from it? Will he be regarded as a 'talented violinist' if he proves unable to follow the score? You know the answer. The best music he will ever play is precisely the music that he was 'created' to play. Remember, the Great Composer knows him, gave him his violin and his talent and He composed the symphony with a special part – to be played only by him.

This violinist can leave the orchestra. He can try to star in his own performance playing his own music with his own violin... but actually, the instrument isn't his. He has stolen it from the Great Composer. He can still play good music with it and be known for his talent. But there are two consequences to consider: 1) he will never play to the best of his ability if he doesn't play the music he was *made for*; and 2) the symphony will never be the same with one less violin. The score was composed counting on his part.

But if I follow the score... am I really free? Of course you are! First of all, because you have to decide to follow the score, *freely* – you could have chosen to play something else. Secondly, because, as you have probably noticed, the same score played by different musicians sounds different. Even the same score played by the same musician sounds different when she is tired, distracted or annoyed. A musician is meant to *interpret* the score. An interpretation is something *personal*. A good musician makes a masterful *interpretation*. But there is no *masterpiece* if the musician doesn't follow the score.

You have a mission. You can choose to fulfil it or not. But even if you choose to fulfil it, you can do it in many ways. A saint is not just someone who *fulfils* his or her mission. A saint, like an artist, is someone who performs their mission as a *masterpiece*!

God is the Conductor of the orchestra and He knows the score of each musician. He is the only one who can understand why your score is as it is. We can perceive that our part is quite dull or simple. But that is because we do not know the whole symphony. And you will not know the symphony until you start playing your score.

Bl John Henry concludes his prayer saying: "*Therefore, I will trust Him, whatever I am, I can never be thrown away ... He does nothing in vain. He knows what He is about. He may take away my friends. He may throw me among strangers. He may make me feel desolate, make my spirits sink, hide my future from me. Still, He knows what He is about.*"

Mary, my Mother, I ask you to intercede for me so that I may have the courage to pray like that.

3

Before the creation of the world

> *"Before I formed you in the womb I knew you, and before you were born I consecrated you; I appointed you a prophet to the nations"* (Jer 1:5).

During a visit to Kazakhstan, St John Paul II said to the young people gathered around him, "*My experience of young people tells me that they are interested in the basic questions. Probably the first question you would want to put to me is this: 'Who am I, Pope John Paul II, according to the Gospel that you proclaim? What is the meaning of my life? Where am I going?' My answer, dear young people, is simple but hugely significant: You are a thought of God, you are a heart-beat of God. To say this is like saying that you have a value which in a sense is infinite, that you matter to God in your completely unique individuality.*"

Some people understand their vocation as a particular calling that God decides at some point in time. It would be like a football coach who observes his players for a long time until eventually he decides to assign them their positions and roles according to their skills. But God doesn't work that way.

Other people think that God is more like a head-hunter, a scout. He has a vacancy, a role to fill in the team and then he scans the market and all the other teams until he finds *the best* for that position in his team. Then, he approaches that player and makes an offer. But the way God acts is very different.

God doesn't need to scout for the right person to fill the gap. God doesn't scan all the different people who could take on a particular role before choosing the best. God creates that player for that role. That player is not just the *best* for that position. He is the *only* option. As they say, he was cut out for it. This is how St Paul puts it: God "*chose us in Christ before the foundation of the world*" (*Eph* 1:4).

A film is a very complex project that involves hundreds of people. When you read the film credits, you find the names of actors and then a whole string of names with roles and jobs that you may find difficult to understand or remember. One of the key people who makes it all happen is the Casting Director. That person is in charge of organising and facilitating the casting of actors for all the roles in a film, finding the ideal artists for each role, as well as arranging and conducting interviews and auditions.

For many, vocation is like that. God needs a priest somewhere so He checks the options, He follows up the candidates and finally, He chooses one. But that is not how vocation works. God is not trying to find you a role in life. He created you and your role together. He made you and wrote the script for you. There is only one candidate for your role, for your vocation: you. You were made for that mission.

The consequences of this line of reasoning are easy to grasp. To begin with, you cannot *choose* your vocation. You *discover* it or you don't, you *follow* it or you don't, but you don't just *'pick one of the options.'* Another consequence is that God can't change His Mind. You can't bargain with Him.

You can, of course, reject the offer – just like a football player can choose not to join that team. All the other team members will have to compensate; they need to fulfil not only their own role but an additional one as well. In the case of the film, if the actor decides not to participate in that film, the director may find another actor; but it won't be the same with your vocation, because the script was written for you and nobody else can read your lines (they would have to change the script as well). Nobody can fulfil a mission that was exclusively designed for you. No one will score your goals or say your lines. Those goals will just never happen. Those lines will never be said.

Another consequence is that you are definitely capable of it. You can't make excuses, saying that it is too much or too little for you, since the mission and the person were thought up together. You, and only you, can do it. God doesn't make mistakes. Whenever you feel like it is too much for you, it may mean that you are not in shape, but it never means that it is not your vocation. Like a football player, talent is not enough. You need grit and training.

So, get to grips with it. God chose you before He decided on the colour of trees and the number of stars and the temperature at which water should boil. He thought about you before He started to build the world you see around you. He loved you then and decided to create you for a particular, exclusive, personal mission that belongs only to you. He then created the world and all that is in it to allow you to fulfil your role.

When you came to exist, everything was ready. There is nothing missing, nothing lacking - except your decision. All you need to become a saint 'your own way', 'your exclusive way' is all set up, waiting for your resolution.

All you need to do is to find your vocation; then, everything will be in your hands…

And you in God's Hands.

A young girl was invited by a friend to help out in a soup kitchen run by the Missionaries of Charity. The first day she was a bit apprehensive, but little by little she found herself more at ease until eventually she thought about her vocation. When she decided to join the Missionaries of Charity, she had to explain it to her mum who was shocked at the news. *"Why do you want to become a nun?"* her mother asked. *"Mum"*, the young girl replied simply, *"I was made for this!"*

Just as Shakespeare was made to write, Lewis Hamilton to race cars and Ed Sheeran to sing, you were also made for something; and your entire life depends on this discovery.

Mary, my Mother, help me to see what God is asking of me; St Joseph, my father and lord, help me to follow God's plans like you did, quickly, as soon as you knew what He was expecting of you.

4

Go to Joseph

> *An angel of the Lord appeared to Joseph in a dream and said, "Joseph son of David, do not be afraid to take Mary home as your wife, because what is conceived in her is from the Holy Spirit. She will give birth to a son, and you are to give him the name Jesus, because he will save his people from their sins." When Joseph woke up, he did what the angel of the Lord had commanded him and took Mary home as his wife. But he did not consummate their marriage until she gave birth to a son. And he gave him the name Jesus. (Mt 1:20-22, 24-25)*

"*Recently I saw in a friend's house a representation of St. Joseph that really made me think*," Pope Benedict XVI explained in a homily: "*It was a relief from a Baroque Portuguese altarpiece, depicting the night of the escape into Egypt. You see an open tent with an angel standing beside it. Inside, Joseph, who is sleeping, but dressed in the garb of a pilgrim, wearing long boots as needed for a difficult journey.*"

It represents St Joseph as a man who is always ready. He could be the man referred to in the Scriptures: "*I slept, but my heart was vigilant*" (*Song* 5:2). St Joseph appears as someone "*whose heart is open enough to receive what the living God and his angel tell him,"* continues the pope. *"In that profound openness, the soul of any man can meet God. From it, God speaks to each of us, and shows that he is close to us... Joseph, as we see, is prompt to get up and do what God tells him, as the Gospel shows us (Mt 1:24; 2:14). This is where his life touches that of Mary, in the response that she gives at the decisive moment of her life: 'Behold, I am the handmaid of the Lord' (Lk 1:38)."*

Pope Benedict XVI recalled the words of Our Lord to St Peter: *"When you were young, you girded yourself and walked where you would; but when you are old, you will stretch out your hands, and another will gird you and carry you where you do not wish to go"* (Jn 21:18). *"Joseph,"* the pope continued, *"with his readiness, makes it his rule of life, because he is ready to let himself be led, even though it is not the direction he wants to go in. His whole life is a story of this kind of responsiveness."*

When Joseph found out that his betrothed was pregnant, all his future plans went down the drain. He was confused about what to do when *"an angel of the Lord appeared to him in a dream"* and explained God's plan to him. God was the Father of that Baby but Joseph had to look after Him and His Virgin Mother. *"When Joseph woke from sleep,"* we read, *"he did as the angel of the Lord commanded him; he took his wife."* It was that simple: he was told to do it, so he woke up and did it.

He prepared the house of Nazareth for the birth of Our Lord and probably built the best crib his hands had ever made. But God suggested a change of plan. This time it wasn't an angel; it was a political affair, a census. Joseph interpreted the situation and did what was expected of him. He took his wife to Bethlehem. There he couldn't find a worthy place for the Son of God to be born. Unable to offer Him what He deserved, Joseph suffered greatly to see the Redeemer lying in a manger; surely he couldn't understand why it should be so.

The Magi came with presents and awakened Herod's jealousy. Again we read that "*an angel of the Lord appeared to Joseph in a dream and said,* '**Rise, take the child and his mother, and flee to Egypt**, *and remain there till I tell you; for Herod is about to search for the child, to destroy him'. And he* **rose** *and* **took the child and his mother** *by night, and* **departed to Egypt**" (Mt 2:13-14). And when we are told that Herod died, the angel made his appearance again with a new commission: "**Rise, take the child and his mother**, *and* **go to the land of Israel**, *for those who sought the child's life are dead*" (Mt 2:20). And what did Joseph do? "*He* **rose** *and* **took the child and his mother**, *and* **went to the land of Israel**" (Mt 2:21).

It is striking how St Matthew describes the actions of Joseph, carrying out immediately (almost word for word) the indications received. That is why the Mass of St Joseph opens with Our Lord's words: '*Behold a faithful and prudent steward whom the Lord set over his household*' (Lk 12:42). He was faithful. There is not a single word of St Joseph's in the Gospels. But there is a great portrait of a faithful man.

Note that Joseph could have rebelled against those things that he didn't understand. How many opportunities he had to say '*This doesn't make any sense*' or '*That is enough!*' After all, was his crib not better than a manger? Was his home in Nazareth not better than a stable in Bethlehem? Why go to Egypt if Nazareth was safe from Herod as well? '*You see?*' Joseph could have argued, '*If we had stayed in Nazareth we wouldn't have to suffer all this!*'

How easily Joseph could have complained about those 'visits' from angels in the middle of the night. '*If God is serious about this plan,*' he could have reasoned, '*the Lord could let me know clearly and distinctively. I think I deserve at least a proper apparition!*' How easily Joseph could have requested a clear proof, a sign, some special confirmation. At the end of the day, he wasn't asked for alms... he was asked for his entire life! He was expected to put his life on the line, to give up everything, to change his plans for the rest of his life. Considering what was at stake, didn't St Joseph deserve clearer instructions or, at least, a chance to ask questions to clarify things more?

That is why Joseph is the saint he is. Some people try to plan their lives down to the smallest detail and won't hear of God suggesting changes to it. Like that lady who had things so perfectly and accurately planned that she wrote her diary a week in advance.

When meditating on their vocation, some people seem to be expecting more proofs and signs and miraculous confirmations than St Joseph. You can be sure they will never come. St Joseph was in tune and could recognise God's voice even in his dreams. He was ready to override his feelings and opinions, to change his plans in order to be perfectly faithful to his mission and to perform it *immediately*, without delay. Let's have it clear in our minds: God will not adapt His plan to ours; we must to adapt our plans to His - if we want.

Mary, how much you loved this *faithful and prudent servant* that God chose to look after you and your Son. Help me to follow St Joseph's example to be open to God's plans for me. Mother, I place myself under your protection and under the powerful intercession of St Joseph, my father and lord, asking for the courage I need to follow God's plan for my life with the same fidelity with which St Joseph heeded Our Lord's Will.

5

In order to be free, choose

"You will know the truth, and the truth will make you free" (Jn 8:32).

We can never talk too much about freedom. Everyone likes to defend freedom. Everyone wants to be free. And yet many people prefer not to have to use it. Because every time you use it and choose something, then you necessarily leave things out of the choice that you will never be able to choose in the future. It's only logical. When my father chose my mother for his wife, he 'chose' to leave many millions of women out of the picture.

You may know the story of that man who was given a very expensive bottle of mature wine as a present. He understood it had to be used for a special occasion. When the wedding of his first daughter was approaching, his wife suggested that he open the bottle. But he refused, arguing that he had other daughters and they might be offended. The man's fiftieth wedding anniversary came up and his wife again suggested opening the wine for the occasion. But he maintained that the fifty-first anniversary would be even more important than the fiftieth, which, in some ways, made sense. To keep it short, after a few years of waiting for a 'special enough event', the man died without tasting it. In the end, his children decided to open the bottle during the reception after his funeral – but they found that the wine had gone off.

Something of the sort happens with freedom. You find people defending their freedom and keeping it safe, but never using it until it is too late. They are afraid to make decisions because they will necessarily discard other options. As Pope Francis wrote, "*The joy of the Gospel, which makes us open to encountering God and our brothers and sisters, does not abide our slowness and our sloth. It will not fill our hearts if we keep standing by the window with the excuse of waiting for the right time, without accepting this very day the risk of making a decision. Vocation is today! The Christian mission is now! Each one of us is called...in order to become a witness of the Lord, here and now.*"

Freedom is like a muscle: *If you don't use it, you lose it*. And the more you use it, the more you get. The problem is that, more often than not, those who don't use their freedom don't know it. When Jesus told the Pharisees that *Truth* could set them free, they laughed at Him – saying that they were perfectly free already. "*We are descendants of Abraham*," they said, "*and have never been in bondage to any one.*"

It is like the bears in the zoo. In their pit, they have trees on which to scratch their backs, an artificial cave as shelter in storms, a pond to take a bath in whenever they feel like it and plenty of food to eat. They may be laughing at you and me, looking down at them from the top of the pit, because we can't take a bath, shelter in their cave, eat their meat or scratch our backs against their trees... They can't see that they are in captivity and that we, who are free, aren't worried about scratching our backs on trees...

Freedom is for something; it's not just freedom for the sake of freedom.

Still, the predominant idea in many people's minds is that if you make a decision, you lose your freedom. Yet, the fact that you are unable to do some things doesn't mean you aren't free. Think again about the bears. The fact that I can't scratch my back on their tree doesn't make me less free.

'But what if I want to? What if I want to scratch my back on the tree?'

'OK. That's fine. Climb into the bear pit. But you may get a few more 'scratches' than you bargained for.'

Are you more free if you jump into the pit? Maybe for a couple of minutes...

Every decision makes you dismiss other options, but in order to keep all options open you have to choose nothing, and to choose *nothing* is not the action of freedom. Imagine a child with a one pound coin standing in front of a vending machine which offers all sorts of snacks. He spends time checking out all the chocolate bars, all the sweets, all the soft drinks... he soon discards a few options he doesn't like but still has 20 different options in front of him. He can spend an hour checking how many milligrams of chocolate or millilitres of drink he can get for one pound. He may go away still holding his coin, afraid of losing it, but he will still be hungry. And licking the coin will not satisfy his cravings.

Yes. Freedom is a risk. Every choice is a risk. And the most important choices in life, the ones that bring real happiness, the ones made for love, are always a risk. But the risk is relative to the person you give yourself to. My mum took a risk when she married my dad. She trusted him and entrusted her happiness to him. He could have come up short... However, you risk nothing when you give yourself to God. He can't come up short.

Peter and James and John and Andrew and the rest of the Twelve took a risk. But what would have become of them if they hadn't? Peter could have become the best fisherman in the Sea of Galilee (which in fact is a lake of 64.4 square miles). He may have held the record for fish caught in one season or won the *"Fisherman of the Year"* award in 30AD. He risked a lot when he left everything in order to follow a Carpenter from Galilee who taught as if He were a rabbi – but with no 'official title.'

As Pope Francis told us in Krakow: *"My friends, Jesus is the Lord of risk, he is the Lord of the eternal "more". Jesus is not the Lord of comfort, security and ease. Following Jesus demands a good dose of courage, a readiness to trade in the sofa for a pair of walking shoes and to set out on new and uncharted paths. To blaze trails that open up new horizons capable of spreading joy, the joy that is born of God's love and wells up in your hearts with every act of mercy. To take the path of the "craziness" of our God...In all the settings in which you find yourselves, God's love invites you to bring the Good News, making of your own lives a gift to him and to others. This means being courageous, this means being free!"*

Mary, my Mother, help me to lose my fear of being truly free, to use my freedom to choose God above all things and entrust myself entirely to Him. My happiness is safe in God's Hands.

6

Great expectations

> *Zechariah asked for a writing tablet, and wrote, "His name is John." And they all marvelled. And immediately his mouth was opened and his tongue loosed, and he spoke, blessing God. And fear came on all their neighbours. And all these things were talked about through all the hill country of Judea; and all who heard them laid them up in their hearts, saying, "What then will this child be?" For the hand of the Lord was with him* (Lk 1:63-66).

The circumstances surrounding the birth of St John the Baptist led people to believe that there was something special about that baby. An elderly couple having a baby, a barren woman giving birth to a son, a mute husband suddenly uttering blessings to God... It was like the magnificent start to a promising film. People in their village couldn't help remembering all this when they saw little John in the streets, walking with his aging parents, wondering again and again, *"What then will this child be?"*

And it would have been a bit disheartening if, in the end, John had become just an average farmer, woodcutter or comedian. It would be a great disappointment for them if the boy had become a scoundrel and a troublemaker, and eventually had failed miserably to live up to their expectations.

Now think about yourself. It is very likely that your mum had the same thought about you when she was holding you on her lap for the first time. She would have looked at you in the form of a tiny baby, unable to do anything except eating and crying (and some other activities that we need not mention here); imagine Mum staring at her newborn baby and wondering, *"what will this child be?"* You can ask her to check how she always had great expectations for you. Yet, however great her expectations were, they will never be as great as God's expectations for you.

It is always sad to see wasted talent, since people never plan to squander their talents. They may fail to use them, usually not because they decide to ignore them, but because they never decide to make them fully fruitful. Perhaps they never get the opportunity they were 'expecting' to have; or they fail to see the real opportunity presented before them.

A baby camel was talking one day with his mum and asking, *"Mum, why have I got these huge three-toed feet?"*

The mother replied, *"Well son, when we trek across the desert your toes will help you to stay on top of the soft sand."*

"Okay," said the son. A few minutes later the son asked, *"Mum, why have I got these great long eyelashes?"*

"They are there to keep the sand out of your eyes on the trips through the desert."

"Thanks, Mum," replied the son. After a short while, the son insists, *"Mum, why have I got these great big humps on my back?"*

The mother, by then a little impatient, replied, *"They are there to help us store fat for our long treks across the desert, so we can go without water for long periods."*

"That's great, mum, so we have huge feet to stop us sinking, and long eyelashes to keep the sand from our eyes and these humps to store water, but Mum..."

"Yes, son?"

"Then... what are we doing in London Zoo?"

Good point! It looks like these camels had a lot of wasted talents.

When figuring out your vocation it is useful to meditate on your talents. God has equipped you with everything you need for your vocation. It's like the main character in an action film. You see Special Agent Ethan Hunt from Mission Impossible, packing his rucksack: a piece of rope, gloves, a torch, a lighter, some explosives, a detonator, a map and a gun. You don't know what's going to happen; but you can be certain of one thing: at some point during the mission they will need a rope and a torch and a map and... We have been 'warned'.

Likewise, when you consider in your prayer your talents, your gifts, your situation, your possibilities... it gives you a glimpse of what God might have had in mind when He made you that way. Nothing is pure chance. Your parents were carefully chosen by God for you for a reason, your brothers and sisters, your nationality, your IQ, your genius, your mother-tongue, your sensitivity, your abilities, your imagination, your creativity... All you have and all you are have been designed by God for a purpose. Checking the contents of your 'rucksack' may give you a clue to the 'mission' you have ahead.

However, this is not an exact science. You need to count on grace and the power of the supernatural. If you think about St Paul, his great intelligence, his mastery of Greek, Latin, Hebrew, Holy Scriptures, even his condition as a Roman citizen, he looks like a very good candidate for apostleship to take the message of the Gospel to Gentiles of all races, places and conditions.

But if you submitted St Peter to this test, he probably wouldn't score highly for the position of prince of the Apostles. On the other hand, Jesus knew Peter's strengths: his character, his determination, his loyalty, his love for Him, his faith; Simon Peter was a man of the world, a hard worker, weather-beaten, seasoned by years of experience.

Knowing your strengths and weaknesses can shed some light on your vocation, but you still need to count on grace. In addition, you need to understand, as we meditated before, that you only have a partial view of yourself. You have to rely on those who know you and know your talents. We will develop this point in the next chapter.

Mary, my Mother, I know that God has great expectations for me; with your intercession, help me to become what God planned for me before He made me as I am.

7

Not me, not me...

> *When they had done this, they caught so many fish that their nets were beginning to break. So they signalled their partners in the other boat to come and help them. And they came and filled both boats, so that they began to sink. But when Simon Peter saw it, he fell down at Jesus' knees, saying, "Go away from me, Lord, for I am a sinful man!" For he and all who were with him were amazed at the catch of fish that they had taken... Then Jesus said to Simon, "Do not be afraid; from now on you will be catching people"* (Lk 5:6-10).

Simon Peter was 'amazed' at the miraculous catch. When he grasped what kind of a Man was in the boat with him, he realised he wasn't up to scratch and we can understand why. A Jewish Rabbi, famous for His preaching, who could perform miracles such as the catch of fish Peter just witnessed surely needed disciples with more qualifications than an illiterate fisherman. Simon Peter had a mental paradigm of what a disciple of Jesus had to be – and he didn't match up to it.

But Jesus told him not to worry. In the parallel texts from St Matthew and St Mark we read that Jesus said to Peter and his companions, "*I will make you fishers of men*" (Mt 4:19; Mk 1:17). It was not Peter who had to *become* a fisher of men. It was Jesus who would *make him* a 'fisher of men.'

That same feeling of inadequacy is present in the vocation of the saints. When you understand the high expectations that God has for you, you necessarily feel a sense of unease, even a sick feeling or a sense of *'vertigo'*. No one thinks he or she is the person for the job. The normal reaction is Peter's one: *'depart from me... I am not the guy.'* And Jesus needed Peter's reaction of humility: a recognition that the job was way beyond his capability. Without humility, you can't become a good instrument in the Hands of God.

That is why that sort of *'vertigo feeling'* is always a good sign. If someone doesn't feel overwhelmed by the vocation God is placing in front of them, that would be a clear sign that they don't understand it well. You never find a cardinal running for the papal election arguing that '*the Church needs a Pope like me'*.

Think of the vocation to the priesthood, for instance. A priest is a man who can forgive sins, anoint the sick, bless marriages, water or whatever he wants to bless; but most importantly, a man who can command God to descend to earth when and where he decides to; a man who can take the Eucharistic God wherever he wants and treat Him as he pleases. So much power, so much responsibility. Yet, if a young lad ever said, '*Priest? Easy peasy, lemon squeezy!*' he would prove he doesn't get it and, therefore, he hasn't got it.

If you ever go to Rome, you can visit the church of San Luigi dei Francesi, near Piazza Navona, which displays the famous masterpiece of Caravaggio, *The Calling of St Matthew*. We could say a lot about the painting but there is no space for it here; you can look it up online. In the picture you can see Jesus pointing his index finger at Matthew, who is sitting at the desk, counting coins with some colleagues. Caravaggio always depicts very expressive characters, dramatic gestures and magnificent contrasts of light and shadow.

I would suggest that you reflect on the three important hands in the painting, all pointing at the same character but in different ways. Jesus' hand is an exact copy of God's hand in the *Creation* by Michelangelo in the Sistine Chapel (it's as if Caravaggio wanted to remind us that every vocation is a re-creation). Jesus seems to be saying, *'That's the man I want!'* Then there is incredulity written on the face of Peter, who is also pointing at Matthew as if asking, *'Are you sure that's the man you want? He is a tax collector!'*

Matthew's facial expression speaks volumes. He is pointing at himself, with his eyes set on Jesus, shocked at the consideration that the Master is calling him, a sinner. It seems as if Peter and Matthew wanted Jesus to reconsider His decision: 'I think you are making a mistake, Jesus. That can't be the man! He is a sinner.' And Our Lord holds fast with determination, still pointing at Matthew, fully aware of who Matthew is.

He could remind Peter of what God said to Samuel when the prophet tried to guess who was the future chosen king: "*The Lord said to Samuel, 'Do not look on his appearance or on the height of his stature...for the Lord sees not as man sees; man looks on the outward appearance, but the Lord looks on the heart'*" (1 *Sam* 16:7).

Don't ever forget that: God knows you better than you do.

You and I can't see ourselves completely. Like a forest, you can walk through it and know it well inside. Someone else can look at it from above and have a clear picture of its limits and surroundings. If you are inside, you can't see the wood for the trees. If you are outside, you can't see each tree, just the forest. That is the vision you have of yourself and the vision that your family and friends can have of you. But God is inside *and* outside. He sees the forest and each tree from the tips to the roots.

So, vertigo is a good sign. It is the understanding that God is demanding a lot. Saints have felt that vertigo. St Teresa of Avila explains about the time when she was a teen: "*Good thoughts about being a nun came to me from time to time, but they soon left me and I could not persuade myself to become one.*" Maybe the best example would be the story of Jonah. When God told him where He wanted him to go, Jonah ran in the opposite direction. That same fear was experienced by Peter, Matthew, St Teresa and Jonah… and it is very understandable.

Mary, my Mother, may I never be afraid of being asked by your Son for more than I think I can give; may I never forget that when God asks for something, He does it with us, within us.

8

Trust

Peter answered him, "Lord, if it is you, bid me come to you on the water." He said, "Come." So Peter got out of the boat and walked on the water and came to Jesus; but when he saw the wind, he was afraid, and beginning to sink he cried out, "Lord, save me." Jesus immediately reached out his hand and caught him, saying to him, "O man of little faith, why did you doubt?" (Mt 14:28-31)

You may be very familiar with this passage of the Gospel. Jesus approaches His disciples walking on the water and Peter makes that odd suggestion of asking Jesus to invite him to do the same. What was Peter thinking? We don't know exactly what was going through his head, but maybe he knew that Jesus could walk on water and his only doubt was whether Jesus could *make someone else* walk on water.

This is a crucial point. We know that Jesus can perform miracles. The problem is, do we trust that He can make *us* perform miracles? Remember His Words: "*Truly, truly, I say to you, he who believes in me will also do the works that I do*." But then He added, "*and greater works than these will he do*." It is a solemn promise ("*Truly, truly, I say to you*") and God always keeps His Word.

45

The crux of Peter's request wasn't whether Jesus could walk on water but whether he himself could do so. We know that Jesus can preach, convert crowds, transform hearts, heal the sick, forgive sins... the question is, can God do that using me as an instrument?

For a moment, Peter thought that God could make him walk on water. But then he doubted and started sinking. When we respond to our vocation we start walking on water; we are doing things that are beyond our capabilities. God transforms lives, brings souls to Him, forgives sins, heals hearts... However, the moment we start doubting, we start sinking.

There is always a great disproportion between what you can do and what God can do in you. What God is asking from His saints is always beyond them. Their vocation was always '*too large*' for them, just as your vocation will be '*too large*' for you. It might seem presumptuous, even a temerity, to say 'Yes'. But it is not. It is quite the opposite: humility. It's the humility to recognise that I can do nothing but God can do everything in me.

As long as you remember that it is not you but Our Lord who does it, then you can walk on water. If you commit the folly of thinking that it's your talents keeping you on the water, you sink. If you don't trust that God can do it, you sink. If you try to do it without Him... you sink.

But even then, when Peter started sinking, he still trusted Jesus enough to ask for help and Jesus took him by the hand and saved him.

A young lad was chatting with the priest about his vocation. He had been praying about it for a while and had come to the realisation that God could be asking him to renounce marriage for something greater. "*However*," he said, "*I don't see myself spending my entire life like you, father. I mean...*"

"*You don't see yourself...?*" repeated the priest. He wasn't offended at all. With a good sense of humour, he patted his belly and said, "*Do you think that when I was your age I saw myself like this?*" All jokes aside, the truth is that nobody can see himself or herself doing what God is asking them to do, because they are not supposed to do it. God does it.

The nun in charge of a hospital ward asked another priest for assistance. There was a patient who was gravely sick and stubbornly refused to go to Confession. After a long conversation the priest left the room having absolved the sins of the repentant dying man. The nun asked in wonder, "*How did you do it, father?*" The priest replied with simplicity, "*I didn't do a thing. Jesus did it. I was just in the way!*"

Remember that: Vocation is not about what *you* can do. It is about what *God can do with you.*

Recall the day when Jesus saw a multitude of five thousand people. The Gospel (*Mt* 14:13-21) tells us that His disciples asked Jesus to dismiss the crowd to allow them to get some food. Jesus said, "*They need not go away; you give them something to eat.*" You can imagine the disciples looking a bit confused, scratching their heads and checking their pockets, wondering how on earth they were supposed to feed that crowd. So they told Jesus, "*We have only five loaves here and two fish.*"

They were absolutely right – they couldn't feed the crowd, unless Jesus did it... through them. So Jesus said to them, "*Bring them here to me.*" And you remember the rest of the story. Jesus could have done the miracle by Himself. But He wanted to use the little they could provide (five loaves and two fish). Our Lord could have distributed the bread and fish Himself, or made it appear in the hands of the people, or ordered some birds to share the pieces out...

They never forgot it. People could eat that day because Jesus multiplied the bread and fish – and they distributed it. So, did they eventually feed the crowd? Yes, they did. But was it really them? Yes, it was: Jesus multiplied, they distributed.

Every vocation is always like that. God asks for something we can't do... without Him. Your vocation will always be like walking on the water and, as long as you trust Him, carrying on the walk. If you doubt, you sink. It will be like distributing the grace that Jesus multiplies.

So yes, there is a lack of proportion between what Jesus asks and what we think we can do. But that is only if you forget that Jesus asks – then He Himself does whatever He asks. You can repeat this prayer of St Augustine: "*O Lord, command what you will and give what you command.*"

Mary, my Mother, may I never forget that my vocation will always be *too large* for me if I try to carry it out by myself, instead of letting Our Lord accomplish it with my help.

9

You have a vocation

> *He chose us in him before the foundation of the world, that we should be holy and blameless before him* (Eph 1:4).

Some people refuse to do anything until they are certain of what God has created them for. They don't want to move in any direction in case they discover later that they have been moving 'away' from where God wanted them to go. In fact, we might not know what God wants from us in the future, but we know for sure what God wants from us *NOW*. He is very specific: "*This is the will of God, your sanctification*" (1 *Thess* 4:3).

God wants us to become saints and we can start now to fulfil that vocation whilst we wait for the next step – when God decides to reveal it to us. Whatever vocation we have, whatever calling God has prepared for us, whatever mission in life, whatever it is, let's be assured that it is included in this one: our vocation to holiness.

As a matter of fact, only if we are trying to live that first vocation are we ready to follow the next instruction. Imagine that you are planning to visit a friend a couple of miles away. You know where the neighbourhood is but you don't happen to know *exactly* how to get there. You type your friend's address into your GPS and it starts 'calculating' the route. After a moment, it indicates that you haven't got any signal. There is no connection yet.

In that situation, you don't have to wait until the navigator has given you the directions to start getting changed. You can put on your trainers and leave the house. Wherever you friend lives, you can start getting close. You know how to get to that neighbourhood. In fact, if your phone hasn't got any signal, you'd better start moving because, precisely when you move your phone will pick up the signal.

Let's get started then!

Whatever plan God has designed for you, it is a fundamental part of your vocation to become a saint. God doesn't call people to become priests but to become saints *as* priests. He doesn't call people to become mothers, but to become saints *by becoming* a wife and a mother. God doesn't need more priests or nuns or mums or dads or lawyers or musicians... God needs holy priests, holy nuns, holy mums and holy dads, holy lawyers and holy musicians. God wants His children to become saints. Any vocation He prepares for His children is a vocation to become a saint following a specific way. Every vocation is a branch in the tree of holiness.

If we want to know what it is exactly that God wants, we need to start moving towards it. Only if we are striving to become a saint can we discover the specific way that God has designed for us to do it. The fact that we don't know the final Will of God doesn't mean that we don't know *anything* about it.

When St Josemaría was 15 he wanted to become an architect and had made his desires clear to his family. He didn't just wake up one day wanting to become a priest. Rather, things began to change starting from the inside. As he explained, "*Our Lord was preparing me in spite of myself, using apparently innocuous things to instil a divine restlessness in my soul. Thus I came to understand very well the love, so human and so divine, that moved Saint Thérèse of the Child Jesus when, leafing through the pages of a book, she suddenly came upon a picture of one of the Redeemer's wounded hands. Things like that happened to me too - things that moved me and led me to daily Communion, to purification, to confession, and to penance."*

Something was brewing inside his heart and, without him being aware of it, he was getting ready to receive his vocation. "*I began to have intimations of Love,*" he explained, "*to realize that my heart was asking for something great, and that it was love. I didn't know what God wanted of me, but it was evident that I had been chosen for something.*"

On Wednesday January 9, 1918, Josemaría turned sixteen. That winter, the city of Logroño lay peacefully under a heavy blanket of snow. As the young man walked through the streets one morning, he looked down and discovered footprints left in the snow. They had been made by a discalced (barefoot) Carmelite friar. Those marks left Josemaría's heart restless. "*If others can make such sacrifices for God,*" he wondered, "*can't I offer Him something?*"

It may seem extraordinary that a little thing like some footprints in the snow was enough to help a teenager make the great decision to give his life to God. But a generous soul, who lives a life of prayer and intimacy with God, can understand the language God often uses to call people who have 'tuned in'.

In fact, young Josemaría perceived that God was asking him to give up his life for something else, but he didn't know what it was. He had 'inklings', he said, that Our Lord was calling him for something he could not yet identify. He understood that becoming a priest would prepare him for whatever God had in store for him. When, on October 2nd 1928 he saw what God wanted from him, he understood why God had been leading him along that path.

As years went by, he could affirm with complete honesty that the beginning of his priestly vocation had been a call from God, a premonition of love, the falling in love of a fifteen- or sixteen-year-old boy.

We all have a vocation. We all have been created for it. We are all called to holiness. And we must start struggling for it now. There is no time to waste. Let's keep moving towards it. Whatever God has planned for us for tomorrow requires us to move towards holiness *now*. So, let's ask ourselves if we are really committed, if we are determined, if we have decided to become saints and have put everything into it. Otherwise, we will be inside our house, with no signal, waiting for the GPS to find the route… but never getting anywhere.

Mary, Mother Most Holy, help me to decide to become a saint. Now! Help me to be determined and to start right now, changing what I need to change, improving what I need to improve, doing what I need to do, praying as I have to pray and trusting God… as you, my Mother, do.

10

Interior disposition

Jesus saw Nathanael coming to him, and said of him, "Behold, an Israelite indeed, in whom is no guile!" (Jn 1:47)

It was the first time Jesus set His Eyes on Nathanael, but He knew his heart. As St John explains in the following Chapter, *"He knew all men and needed no one to bear witness of man; for he himself knew what was in man"* (Jn 2:25). Jesus knew what was in Nathanael's heart and so the Master knew he was then ready to follow Him. To be ready doesn't mean that he couldn't say 'No'. When Our Lord made the same offer to the rich young man – *"Jesus, looking upon him, loved him"* (Mk 10:21) – the young man said 'No'.

Jesus knew what was in his heart as well. If the Lord called him it was because He could see the young man was 'ready', able to say 'Yes'. However, the youth decided to reject the offer. In other words, to be 'ready' means to be able to say 'Yes'. Conversely, because he is free, he is able to say 'No'.

Some people think that what really matters is to *know* what God wants from you, independent of what your answer to that calling would be. Now, that is not entirely correct. If someone is not ready to say 'Yes', they are not yet ready to receive the call.

Vocation is a mission that God prepared for us when He thought about us before the creation of the world. We were created for something. That mission is there from the beginning but God does not disclose it from the beginning. He does not even disclose it in one go. Someone once described our vocation as a hostage-taking situation. We can think of our vocation as if it had been *kidnapped* by God. In our prayer we need to negotiate, to come to terms with God for the release of our *hostage mission*.

For that negotiation to take place, *goodwill* is indispensable. When disclosing our mission, God acts like a young man who wants to propose to his fiancée. That is a decisive moment that he cannot improvise. The fiancé prepares the occasion as best he can: time, place, words… Some things will be out of his control and he has to just play it by ear, but there is one indispensable thing that he will never forget to take into account; something he will always consider first, acting only once he has made sure of it: He will never propose to his fiancée until he is reasonably certain that *she is willing to say 'Yes'*.

He will never propose to her in a moment when she is upset with him or feeling miserable after failing an exam or disappointed with him because he forgot her birthday… We would all agree that those are not the best moments for a marriage proposal.

God also considers our willingness before He reveals to us our vocation – which is also a proposal, a declaration of love. If He sees that we are not very willing or ready to say 'Yes' to His offer, He might decide to wait. That is why we need to start with a chapter on *interior dispositions*. For negotiations with God it is absolutely essential to convince Him that we are willing to do *whatever* He wants us to do. In our prayer we can go through the different options and say: *"Lord, if You were to ask me 'this'... I'd say 'Yes'; if, on the other hand, You were to ask me 'that'... my answer would also be 'Yes'."* Until God hears that 'music' it is unlikely that He will disclose His plans for us.

But we must be honest. Do not say 'Yes' when you feel like saying 'No'. Sincerity is essential in this negotiation. Therefore, sometimes our prayer might be more like: *"Lord, if You ask me 'this'... I will say 'Yes'; but if you ask me 'that'... Well, Lord, if You really want me to do 'that', You may have to give me special graces, because right now I don't feel like saying 'Yes' to that..."*

That is a disposition of trust. I don't feel like accepting it, but I trust in God my Father and know that He would never propose a vocation for me that wasn't the best for me. So, if my Father God was asking me to do something I feel incapable of doing, I would remind Him that I trust in Him and ask Him to make the changes necessary for me to be able to say 'Yes'.

A football player had a serious injury. It was a second team with very young players and he was an important defender with great responsibility. After an evaluation of the injury, it was clear that the lad would not be able to play for the rest of the season. The coach had no one else ready to play in his position, so he called a meeting with the trainer and the captain of the team to decide the best course of action. After going through the different options, they realised that the best player for that position was the captain himself, but he had never played in that position before. The coach asked the captain, *"Do you think you are ready to play in his position?"*

The youngster wasn't the captain by chance. He was a boy with drive and determination – he was committed. After a moment of reflection, he replied, *"I'm not ready, sir. I have never played there."* But before anyone could say anything, he turned to the trainer and added, "*You, sir, make me ready!*" That season he proved to be the best player in that new position. It was in this new position that he became a well-known player in the first division. It took time and effort… but he was *ready* to be made '*ready*'.

God can make us ready. If we pray like that, if we are honest and ask Him to prepare us, to make us ready, we will be able to say 'Yes' with His grace. This is a good prayer:

Mary, my Mother, help me to say 'Yes' to anything God wants of me; St Joseph, my father and Lord, make me love the Will of God; my Guardian Angel, help me to do whatever God wants.

11

Blank cheque

> *As they were going along the road, a man said to him, "I will follow you wherever you go." And Jesus said to him, "Foxes have holes, and birds of the air have nests; but the Son of man has nowhere to lay his head." To another he said, "Follow me." But he said, "Lord, let me first go and bury my father." But he said to him, "Leave the dead to bury their own dead; but as for you, go and proclaim the kingdom of God." Another said, "I will follow you, Lord; but let me first say farewell to those at my home." Jesus said to him, "No one who puts his hand to the plough and looks back is fit for the kingdom of God"* (Lk 9:57-62).

Reading these conversations, we get the impression that Jesus wasn't making it easy for those people to follow Him. It could even seem like He was trying to dissuade them. However, the truth is that Jesus was being perfectly honest and open. He didn't want anyone to follow Him having the wrong expectations; following Christ always means going uphill.

When we try to come to terms with God we need to be aware that He is a tough negotiator. He does not compromise. Here it is *all-or-nothing*. There are things in life with which you can bargain. If you go to buy bananas, you can buy one, three or a dozen, according to your will or your budget. If you want to buy a car, your options are reduced to a few. You can choose the colour, the radio, the upholstery and a few other features, but you cannot ask for half of the car or just the car without an engine or with only one seat if you do not have enough money to pay for it. You take the whole car or you don't take it at all.

Imagine how ridiculous a conversation would be if someone tried to bargain for something that is not up for negotiation: *'Would you like to be my wife from Fridays to Sundays for the rest of your life?'* Or *'OK, I'll marry you, but I'll go and stay with my parents for one week every month to get a break from you...'* Those are not terms for negotiation. The same thing applies to the person we are. If someone is your mother, she is not your mother only for a few days or a few years. Consider the absurdity of this exchange:

- 'Sorry, madam, is that your child?'

- 'Yeah, well, sometimes!'

It doesn't make any sense.

We could use the same approach when talking about duties: you will not see a train driver divert the train to bring his wife the eggs and butter that she urgently needs to cook his dinner. Nor would you see the driver stop the train and announce over the loudspeaker that he has to take a nap (right now!) because he had a bad night…

In the text that we read at the beginning of the chapter, Jesus asked a young man to follow Him and the fellow replied, *"Lord, let me first go and bury my father"* (Lk 9:59). He didn't say, 'No'; instead he said, *'I will, but first I have other plans…'* Jesus asked him to leave everything and to forget his personal plans. A few metres along the road another fellow volunteered, *"I will follow you, Lord; but let me first say farewell to those at my home"* (Lk 9:61).

Again, someone who wanted to lay down his own conditions. Jesus' answer was firm: *"No one who puts his hand to the plough and looks back is fit for the kingdom of God" (Lk 9:62).* You can't say 'Yes' to God and then try to put a personal project before your calling.

One day, St Josemaría met a young boy who was thinking about giving his life entirely to God. But his reasoning was too negative: *"If I say 'Yes'",* he was arguing, *"then I won't be able to do this anymore... If I did, would I have to give up this and that...?"* St Josemaría answered, *"Here, we don't bargain with the Lord... the invitation of the Lord is something you either take or leave, just as it is. You need to make up your mind: go forward, fully decided and without holding back; otherwise, go away ... 'Whoever is not with Me, is against Me'" (Mt 12:30).*

Trying to negotiate with God to reduce our commitment or reach a compromise just will not work. We cannot haggle over our vocation with God. We are free to either accept it or reject it, but we can't change it. "If you are in, you are in." God never settles for less than 'everything'.

Hence the concept of the blank cheque is used often to describe our acceptance of God's calling. People write a blank cheque when they don't know the exact amount they have to write. The cheque is signed but has no figures on it. It is risky because if we lose that cheque, someone can write whatever number they want and get all that money from our account.

If you currently had £10,000 in your account, that would be the maximum amount of money anyone could take from you now. However, imagine that the person who got the cheque kept it in a safe for a while. You keep adding money to your account, saving to buy the house of your dreams. One day, when you manage to save £400,000 for the house, the person who had the cheque in his possession could take all that money out. That gives you an idea of how much you risk when signing a blank cheque.

So it is with God. He knows all that we have and all that we will be able to have in the future. And He asks for it all.

When God asks someone to follow Him, He is asking for that blank cheque. He is not just asking for everything that we have right now; He is asking also for everything that we will have in the future. God is not interested only in what we are now but also in what we will be. God knows our talents, our skills, our inclinations, our passions, our interests, our projects, our ambitions... He also knows our miseries, our mistakes, selfishness and sins. And He asks for it all.

That's the greatness of our vocation. God counts on what we are and on what we will become. Therefore, it is necessary to decide in our prayer whether we are ready to give it all – or whether we feel like bargaining with Him. Our vocation is not a part-time job or a society or charity that you can join as a volunteer in your free time. God needs us all and He needs the whole of us.

Now it is time to think about my disposition. Am I ready to allow God to write any figure He thinks I can give? Honestly, if God calls you to celibacy in the middle of the world, or to become a priest, or a nun, or a missionary, or a Capuchin friar or a husband-father of 12 children... are you ready to say 'Yes'?

Mary, my Mother, through your intercession, help me to be able to accept God's terms without hesitation. St Joseph, show me how to follow God's plan. My Guardian Angel, give me a push when I need it.

12

Committing without knowing the consequences?

> *As he walked by the Sea of Galilee, he saw two brothers, Simon who is called Peter and Andrew his brother, casting a net into the sea; for they were fishermen. And he said to them, "Follow me, and I will make you fishers of men." Immediately they left their nets and followed him* (Mt 4:18-20).

They left everything, signed their blank cheque and followed Him. They didn't know where they were going, whether they were going to come back or even what this *'fishers-of-men thing'* was supposed to mean. But that didn't stop them.

Some people are afraid to say 'Yes' to God's plan because they don't know to what they are really committing themselves. How can someone at the age of 14 promise to fulfil a mission without knowing exactly what will be demanded in the future? The answer is quite simple: God only asks what we can give. If He asks a 14-year-old girl to give her life to Him, like St Thérèse of Lisieux, it is because He is expecting from her what a 14-year-old girl can give. Previously she had let God know that she wanted to do His Will in everything. She didn't know what the future would bring – and she didn't care.

After all, is there any situation in life that can be completely predictable? A husband marries his wife without knowing whether she will have any illness in the future or whether she can bear children, whether his job will be stable or whether they will always live in the same house or city, whether they will have a sick child... so many things can happen in the future! But that doesn't stop him from committing his future to that woman.

In the end, we trust in the Person who has chosen us. That husband could go crazy and leave his wife, but God is faithful. He doesn't fail. If He gives a vocation, He gives the grace we need to carry it out and He stays at our side all the way.

Bl Cardinal Newman had difficulties following God's call to convert to Catholicism. His conversion to the Church of Rome opened for him a very gloomy prospect. His family didn't support him; he lost his job as an Anglican pastor, his income and his position in Oxford University. He had nothing to rely on except God who was calling him to take that last step. In this frame of mind he wrote one of his most famous poems, *Lead, Kindly Light*. As a prayer, he asks God to lead his steps along whatever path God might want to take him, as long as He leads him 'home': "*Lead, Kindly Light, amidst th'encircling gloom, Lead Thou me on!*" He explains how he feels the darkness around him and has no other light to guide him than the Light of God: "*The night is dark, and I am far from home, Lead Thou me on! Keep Thou my feet...*" But then he asks for help to see not the distant future and all that is ahead; he asks to see just enough to take one more step: "*I do not ask to see the distant scene; one step enough for me.*"

Just one more step is enough. Saints didn't demand to see what was ahead. They knew that God was always ahead of them. It was enough for them to know that God was taking care of that and He would only bring what is best for His children. When St Teresa of Calcutta said 'Yes' to God at the age of 12, she couldn't possibly know to what exactly she was saying 'Yes'. God never gives the whole picture at the beginning, just as films don't tell you the ending right at the start. God always shows what He wants now and expects that we do it now.

Jesus said it clearly, "*Therefore do not be anxious about tomorrow, for tomorrow will be anxious for itself. Let the day's own trouble be sufficient for the day*" (*Mt* 6:34). God wants us to trust Him. Like a GPS or Sat-Nav, God doesn't give all the instructions for the journey in one go, but step by step; otherwise it would be very overwhelming, wouldn't it?

St John Bosco said once, "*Had I known all the problems and difficulties that this institution was going to give me, I wouldn't have dared to try to do it.*" And St Josemaría commented in a conversation with a group of people, "*If I had known in 1928 what was in store for me, I would have died. But God our Lord treated me as a child. He did not lay the burden on me all at once, but led me onward little by little. A little child is not given four things to do at once. First he's given one and then another; and then another, when he has done the previous one. Have you seen a little boy playing with his father? The boy has some wooden blocks, of different shapes and colours... And his father tells him: 'Put this one here, and that one there, and the red one over there.' And he ends up with a castle!*"

Never forget it: *God is our Father*. A good father will never be content with his child being mediocre. A good father will always encourage his children to develop their talents from the beginning. When the child is 7, he can be asked what a 7-year-old boy can give. When the child is 15, he can be expected to do what a 15-year-old man can cope with. As a good Father, God never asks for more than we can give; but He never asks us for less. All He asks is that we trust in Him and allow Him to lead our steps.

Lead, Kindly Light, amidst th'encircling gloom,

Lead Thou me on!
The night is dark, and I am far from home,
Lead Thou me on!
Keep Thou my feet; I do not ask to see
The distant scene; one step enough for me.

I was not ever thus, nor prayed that Thou
Shouldst lead me on;
I loved to choose and see my path; but now
Lead Thou me on!
I loved the garish day, and, spite of fears,
Pride ruled my will. Remember not past years!

So long Thy power hath blest me, sure it still
Will lead me on.
O'er moor and fen, o'er crag and torrent, till
The night is gone,
And with the morn those angel faces smile,
Which I have loved long since, and lost awhile!

Meantime, along the narrow rugged path,
Thyself hast trod,
Lead, Saviour, lead me home in childlike faith,
Home to my God.
To rest forever after earthly strife
In the calm light of everlasting life.

Mary, Virgin Most Faithful, may I learn with your help to trust my Father God, Who only wants the best for me. St Joseph, my father and lord, help me to abandon myself into the Hands of Our Lord. My Guardian Angel, help me to simplify my life, so that I can be like a little child before God.

13

I can't ðo this!

> *When Simon Peter saw it, he fell down at Jesus' knees, saying, "Depart from me, for I am a sinful man, O Lord." For he was astonished, and all that were with him, at the catch of fish which they had taken; and so also were James and John, sons of Zebedee, who were partners with Simon. And Jesus said to Simon, "Do not be afraid; henceforth you will be catching men." And when they had brought their boats to land, they left everything and followed him (Lk 5:8-11).*

The first prayer that Peter ever said, the first request he made of Our Lord was to ask Jesus to depart from him and leave him behind. St Peter couldn't understand why any rabbi could be interested in a fisherman to make of him a disciple. However, Jesus wasn't any rabbi. He was the Son of God. A rabbi could be mistaken. But not God. Our Lord knew what was in his heart (Jn 2:25).

Anyone who is introduced to a vocation will instantly object that it is too much for them; that they are not the right person, that they are unable, incapable, unqualified for the mission. Well, of course they are! A supernatural vocation is, by definition, beyond our human resources. A 'supernatural' calling is always beyond 'natural' means. Think about the universal vocation to holiness. To become a medical doctor you need to study, to practise, to spend time and money and, eventually, you get your degree. That's within human reach.

However, to be holy is not just a matter of doing things. You need to be *'made holy'* by God's grace. When God calls, He is asking for 'permission' to make something supernatural with you, in you. If He wants a young man to be a priest He would ask him: *'Would you like me to make of you a holy priest and save many souls with your help?'* That is the same as saying: *'I want you to be a priest. What do you say?'*

When talking about vocation there is an important idea that should always be remembered: *God does not call the equipped. He equips the called.* He didn't appoint Peter the Prince of the Apostles for his eloquence, his attractive personality, his leadership qualities and sympathy... Moses had to run away from Egypt because he had murdered an Egyptian (he was a murderer!) One day he was pasturing his father-in-law's flock and saw the burning bush that wasn't consumed. It was like bait from God. For when Moses saw it, he approached to check why it wasn't consumed.

Then God talked to Moses from the bush and explained to him that he had been chosen to save the people of Israel and lead them out of Egypt. From what we read, it looks like Moses preferred to lead sheep and cattle rather than Israelites, because he tried to decline the offer. Moses said to Our Lord, "*Who am I that I should go to Pharaoh, and bring the sons of Israel out of Egypt?*" (*Ex* 3:11). In other words, *'I'm not the guy; you need someone else'*. God then tried to put Moses' mind at rest, explaining that He Himself would be with him and everything would be fine. But Moses still wasn't convinced. He replied, "*But behold, they will not believe me or listen to my voice.*" God then gave him the sign of the rod. When Moses cast his rod on the ground it became a serpent. That was a visible sign. God had performed a miracle, which was impossible to deny.

Everything seemed settled then, but Moses still wasn't very willing to follow God's instructions since he insisted, "*Oh, my Lord, I am not eloquent, either heretofore or since thou hast spoken to thy servant; but I am slow of speech and of tongue*"(*Ex* 4:10). Apparently Moses had a speech impediment and stuttered. God then gave the best answer to those who think they are not up to par with their vocation when He said to Moses, "*Who has made man's mouth? Who makes him dumb, or deaf, or seeing, or blind? Is it not I, the Lord? Now therefore go, and I will be with your mouth and teach you what you shall speak*" (*Ex* 4:11-12). In other words: 'I, God, made you as you are because I needed you for this mission.'

It wasn't a mistake. Moses stammered because God made him stammer. The mission did not depend on Moses' voice but on him allowing God to perform his miracles through him. His mission wasn't to convince Pharaoh with eloquent words. It was to do what God asked for and deliver His message. Moses still wasn't ready to budge: "*Oh, my Lord, send, I pray, some other person*." But God drives a hard bargain, and eventually saved His People with Moses and not with someone else.

That is the greatness of our vocation: God could have saved His People without Moses. God could have converted Nineveh without Jonah. God could have transformed the Roman Empire without Peter and Paul. He could have reached the poor Italian immigrants in America without St Frances Cabrini and the slums of Calcutta without St Teresa. God could have reached the people of China without St Francis Xavier and comforted the lepers of Molokai without St Damien... Meditate on this in depth: *God could do in an instant all that I am supposed to do during my entire life; and He could do it without me!*

God could have converted Ireland on His own, but He wanted to add St Patrick's name to that achievement. God did convert Ireland; and He did it with St Patrick. That's the privilege of the saints. Like a co-author, God wants to put the name of a saint next to His in any enterprise. And now He wants your name and mine, next to His, in this particular mission He has for you and for me. Vocation is a privilege, not a duty.

Feeling that we are not ready for a particular vocation is necessary. Not even Our Lady was ready to be the Mother of God: how can a creature be Mother of the Creator? When St Gabriel announced the Incarnation to her she was perplexed. But she asked just one thing, *'What am I supposed to do?'* And the answer was simple: *'Just say "Yes" and the Holy Spirit will do it'*. All you have to do is to say 'Yes'.

That's what Moses did, and Jonah and Peter and Paul, and Frances and Teresa and Xavier and Damien and Patrick... They said 'Yes' - and God did all the rest.

Mary, Queen of the Apostles, St Joseph, my father and lord, my Guardian Angel, help me to say a quick and firm 'Yes' to whatever Our Lord has prepared for me. I want to be the co-author of His great plan for the two of us.

14

Should I volunteer?

> *I heard the voice of the Lord saying, "Whom shall I send, and who will go for us?" Then I said, "Here am I! Send me." And he said, "Go, and say to this people: Hear and hear, but do not understand; see and see, but do not perceive"* (Is 6:8-9).

During the History of Salvation, God called different people to become His prophets. They were sent by Him to warn His people, to teach them, to give them hope and sometimes to perform miracles. But all the prophets had a difficult time and many of them died as martyrs. Often the People of Israel were not willing to listen to them or to do what they said. The calling of Isaiah is a particularly good example. In chapter 6 of his Book he recounts a vision of God on a throne surrounded by His Angels. Overwhelmed by this vision, Isaiah is purified by an Angel and then the Voice of the Lord resounds: *"Whom shall I send, and who will go for us?"* (Is 6:8). It surprises us to see God surrounded by all kinds of powerful Angels and still asking for a volunteer. It is striking that, instead of sending someone, God asks if anyone wants to undertake this mission.

This is how God acts. He could, of course, make everyone do what He knows is best. But that is not His policy. God always asks. He always gives us the choice. We are always free, because without our freedom we would not be able to please Him. So, going back to the text of the prophet, Isaiah heard God's request and answered straight away: "*Here am I! Send me.*" What about the Angels present in the vision? Are they not more powerful, more diligent, more capable of fulfilling this mission than Isaiah? At the end of the day, that has been their mission for centuries... The very word 'angel' means 'messenger'. Why would you send a man if you can send a Seraphim or an Archangel?

It brings to mind the Council of Elrond, in the first book of '*The Lord of the Rings*'. Different creatures are gathered there to decide the fate of the Ring: skilled elves, powerful men, strong dwarfs... even a wise and mighty wizard! Bilbo makes the point that the Council should appoint the one who is to take the Ring to Mordor. There is silence in the air. No one dares to speak. '*Frodo glanced at all the faces, but they were not turned to him,*' Tolkien writes. '*All the Council sat with downcast eyes, as if in deep thought. A great dread fell on him, as if he was awaiting the pronouncement of some doom that he had long foreseen and vainly hoped might after all never be spoken. An overwhelming longing to rest and remain at peace by Bilbo's side in Rivendell filled all his heart. At last with an effort he spoke, and wondered to hear his own words, as if some other will was using his small voice.*

"*I will take the Ring,*" *he said,* "*though I do not know the way*".'

We can't help feeling grateful to the brave little hobbit. Elrond speaks our thoughts in Tolkien's novel: '*Elrond raised his eyes and looked at him, and Frodo felt his heart pierced by the sudden keenness of the glance.* "*If I understand aright all that I have heard,*" *he said,* "*I think that this task is appointed for you, Frodo; and that if you do not find a way, no one will. This is the hour of the Shire-folk, when they arise from their quiet fields to shake the towers and counsels of the Great. Who of all the Wise could have foreseen it? Or, if they are wise, why should they expect to know it, until the hour has struck?"'*

Vocation is always a personal enterprise that affects the world, a personal task that nobody can do for us. As Elrond says, if Frodo doesn't find a way, "*no one will.*" The world needs us to take a step forward and prepare ourselves for the task we were chosen for by God.

We are always free to accept. Elrond himself explains this point to Frodo: '"*But it is a heavy burden. So heavy that none could lay it on another. I do not lay it on you. But if you take it freely, I will say that your choice is right".*' Frodo is not a warrior, he is not strong, he is not skilled or wise. But we have learned something about him in the first part of the book: He is not a coward. He is not ambitious. He is honest. He is faithful.

As it appears in that novel, so it is in real life. Vocation can't be imposed on anyone. It is a heavy burden that surpasses our faculties. Saints have always been, like Frodo, little creatures playing a role bigger than themselves, knowing they are backed by God Himself - Who covers the backs of those appointed instruments in His plan of salvation.

To fulfil the mission that God has thought up for us, we do not need anything else than to accept it. Because inside the same pack in which we get our mission, we always get the grace we need to carry it forward. And, as in '*The Fellowship of the Ring*', you will never walk alone. God is with you all the time, giving you courage, instructions, energy, grace...

To answer the question that opened this chapter, should you volunteer? Yes. God needs to know that He can count on you. In your prayer you can consider the different options that lie open before you and, one by one, tell Our Lord that if that is His Will, it is also yours. '*Lord,*' you can say to Him in your prayer, '*if You want me to become a* [fill the gap here], *You can count on me!*

If, on the other hand, You prefer me to become a [again, fill the gap]*, then I prefer that option also. If you are considering asking me to do this other thing* [fill this gap also]*, well, let's be honest, Lord, that would cost me a bit more, really... I don't think I can do that, but if You think I can, it's settled - with Your help, I will say "Yes".'*

You can keep going like that, considering the many options that you think God has put in front of you for your reflection. If you have doubts as to whether you would be suitable for a particular vocation, you can always ask your spiritual director. If you don't have one, find one – you really need one.

You can say like the prophet Isaiah, "*Here am I! Send me.*" Or even better, like Our Lady, Virgin Most Faithful, "*Behold the handmaid of the Lord, be it done unto me according to your Word.*" St Joseph, help me have those words on my lips all the time. My Guardian Angel, remind me of them often.

15

What if I simply can't say 'Yes'?

> *Now the word of the Lord came to Jonah the son of Amit'tai, saying, "Arise, go to Nin'eveh, that great city, and cry against it; for their wickedness has come up before me." But Jonah rose to flee to Tarshish from the presence of the Lord. He went down to Joppa and found a ship going to Tarshish; so he paid the fare, and went on board, to go with them to Tarshish, away from the presence of the Lord* (Jon 1:1-3).

We are too familiar with the story of Jonah. When God delivered him his mission, he ran away. He just wasn't ready. It took God a while and a bit of effort to make him 'reconsider' his attitude. We may find ourselves in this situation. When we know what God may have chosen for us but we don't really feel like saying *'Yes'* or at least, not wholeheartedly. Instead of a *'Yes'* we may be more inclined to say *'Oooo-kay'*.

Kimberly Hahn was a Presbyterian when Scott, her husband, converted to Catholicism. She narrates a conversation she had with her father at the time when she started thinking about becoming a Catholic herself. All reason pointed towards the plenitude of the faith within the Catholic Church, but her heart resisted with all its might and prevented her from taking the final step. She was suffering an interior crisis very similar to that of people who are deciding whether to give themselves up to God: she saw clearly the path she needed to take but her heart and will were resisting it.

Kimberly writes: *A little before our daughter was born, I had an important conversation with my father. He is one of the holiest men I know. In truth, he was the father I needed to guide me towards my Heavenly Father. He detected the sadness in my voice and asked me:*

"Kimberly, do you pray the prayer I say every day? Do you say: "Lord, I will go where you want me to go, I will do what you want me to do, I will say what you want me to say, and I will give up what you want me to give up?"

"No, Daddy, during these days I have not said that prayer."

He had no idea about the agony I had been going through since the conversion of Scott to the Catholic faith. And he answered me, disturbed: "You are not saying it!"

"Daddy, I'm scared to say it. I am scared to pray it because that prayer could mean that I will have to join the Roman Catholic Church. And I will never be a Roman Catholic!"

"Kimberly, I do not think that the prayer means that you have to convert. What it means is that either Jesus is the Lord of all your life or He is not your Saviour at all. You do not tell the Lord where you want or do not want to go. What you are telling Him is that you are there for Him. This is what disturbs me even more than the fact that you may become a Roman Catholic. You are hardening your heart against the Lord. If you cannot recite this prayer, then ask God for the grace to say it, until you finally have the strength to say it out loud. Open your heart to Him: you can trust Him."

He was risking a great deal when he said that.

For 30 days, I prayed: "Lord, give me the grace to say this prayer." I was scared that by praying it, I would be sealing my destiny: I would have to get rid of my capacity to think, forget everything that was in my heart, and follow Scott like an imbecile towards the Catholic Church.

Finally I found myself ready to pray, putting all the consequences in the hands of Our Lord. What I discovered then was that I myself had created a cage around me, and that Our Lord had opened the doors to set me free, instead of locking me up and throwing away the key. My heart was thumping. Now I was free to study and understand, to begin to examine things once again, but this time, with a sense of joy. Very well, Lord, I have realized that these were not the plans for my life, but that Your plans are better for me. What do You want to do with my heart? In my marriage? In our family?" [Scott and Kimberly Hahn, *Rome Sweet Home* (San Francisco: 2000)].

Jonah could have started with that prayer instead of running away as soon as he realised what God was asking him to do. Instead of God making him 'reconsider' his attitude, Our Lord would have given him the grace he needed to accept his vocation and do it wholeheartedly.

Some people, when thinking about their vocation, may have to start by saying a prayer similar to that one. '*I don't think am ready yet... Lord, You make me ready!*' In every important decision in life we need to prepare ourselves to make the best choice. To prepare ourselves to say 'Yes' to God we need to have a personal relationship with Him. We need an intense life of prayer. We need to love God before we are able to give Him our lives and decide to spend the rest of our lives with Him. And that requires preparation.

Therefore, one of the first steps in the process of discerning our vocation is asking God for the grace we need to be able to say 'Yes' to Him, to follow Him wherever He wants to take us. Remember St Joseph when he found out that Mary was pregnant: he was utterly confused. He didn't run away, like

Jonah. Instead, he started pondering, considering all the options, praying and meditating about it. So when the angel came to disclose his mission, he was ready to accept it straight away and to do what God wanted him to do.

You can ask the help of Our Lady, St Joseph and your Guardian Angel to be able to say that prayer with its full meaning: *"Lord, I will go where you want me to go, I will do what you want me to do, I will say what you want me to say, and I will give up what you want me to give up."*

16

Getting ready

> *Jesus said to him, "One thing you still lack. Sell all that you have and distribute to the poor, and you will have treasure in heaven; and come, follow me." But when he heard this he became sad, for he was very rich* (*Lk* 18:22).

As other rabbis did, Jesus went around Judea and Galilee calling those He wanted. Some had followed Him for a while, listened to His preaching and seen His miracles before He called them to be closer to Him. As St Mark describes it, Jesus '*appointed twelve, whom he also named apostles, to be with him, and to be sent out to proclaim the message*' (Mk 3:14).

Peter and Andrew were mending their nets when Jesus approached them and called them. '*And immediately,*' the Gospel says, '*they left their nets and followed him*' (Mark 1:18). A few moments later Jesus saw James and John, who were in their boat. '*Immediately,*' we are told again, '*He called them; and they left their father Zebedee in the boat with the hired men, and followed him.*'

We read the same about St Matthew: '*As he walked along, he saw Levi son of Alphaeus sitting at the tax collector's booth. "Follow me," Jesus told him, and Levi got up and followed him.*'

They seem to be very simple interactions. God called them; they said 'Yes'. But that didn't happen all the time. Reading the story of the rich young man, you find the same call but a very different response (*Mt* 19:16-30). Peter, Andrew, James and John had to leave their boats and nets; Matthew had to leave his business. This young man also had to give up his possessions. But he wasn't ready.

We are told that he lacked just one thing. "*If you would be perfect,*" Jesus says (*Mt* 19:21); '*But only **if you wish**...*' - because the answer to the calling of God is always free. "*You lack **one thing**,*" Our Lord tells the young man. Just one! "*Go,*" Jesus tells him, "*sell what you have, and give to the poor, and you will have treasure in heaven; and come, follow me*" (*Mk* 10:21). But that 'one thing' was enough to prevent him from following Jesus. So, he "*became sad,*" and we could add that he remained sad until he decided to sort out that 'one thing' and follow Jesus.

To be able to say 'Yes' to your vocation you need to get spiritually fit.

A mum was tidying up her son's room when she came across a list of virtues pinned inside his wardrobe. The list included: Charity, study, prayer, humility, obedience, service, reliability, steadiness, goodness... There were ticks and crosses on the list. She became curious and in the evening she asked her son where he got the list from and why was it there. The 15-year-old boy explained that someone asked the parish priest during their catechism lessons 'what was needed to become a saint.' Those were some of the virtues the priest mentioned. We can tell he was 'getting ready' for something!

To say 'Yes' to God we must be able to give not just many things, but to give ourselves. And we cannot give what we do not possess. We must first possess ourselves to be able to give ourselves away.

The young boy's plan is a good example to follow. Like a professional football player, you need a plan to improve. The player knows his strengths and weaknesses. With his trainer, he can prepare a plan to work on those aspects that need improvement and that can change his game. There may be many things to improve, but some are more important than others.

Professional athletes need a coach who can watch them perform and point out the things they need to improve. They say that *'four eyes are better than two'*. But the best eyes to spot these problems are always someone else's eyes. Professional athletes can't see themselves performing. They miss many things they do wrong when they are in the thick of the game. In order to improve, they need a coach; one who spots problems, addresses issues, provides advice, encourages players when they go through a difficult patch; someone they can rely on.

In the spiritual life, our coach is the spiritual director or spiritual guide. Someone who knows us, can give us advice and encourage us when things get difficult. The spiritual guide can know us because we tell them what is going on in our souls. As with a doctor, we need total sincerity with the spiritual director.

In 2014, tennis player Garbiñe Muguruza had had steady results but wasn't yet a top player. In 2015 she hired a new coach, Sam Sumyk, because, as she put it, she could do much better but needed to be 'challenged'. The following year she won her first Grand Slam and became World number 2. In 2017, she won the Wimbledon tournament and rose to number 1 in the WTA rankings. She was right to seek challenge!

We could apply this to spiritual guidance. Apart from telling our spiritual directors the truth, we need to allow them to make demands on us, to challenge us. They can help us identify our weak points, the main obstacles that prevent us from fulfilling

Gods Will. They can give us direction, can tell us which aspects of our life we need to work on and how to do it. Ultimately, a spiritual director is someone who can follow up our progress. Without a plan there is no improvement.

Holy Mary, my Mother, show me the things that God wants me to change. St Joseph, my father and lord, help me to change them. My Guardian Angel, let's do this together!

17

Prepare the soil

> *"A sower went out to sow. And as he sowed, some seeds fell along the path, and the birds came and devoured them. Other seeds fell on rocky ground, where they had not much soil, and immediately they sprang up, since they had no depth of soil, but when the sun rose they were scorched; and since they had no root they withered away. Other seeds fell upon thorns, and the thorns grew up and choked them. Other seeds fell on good soil and brought forth grain, some a hundredfold, some sixty, some thirty. He who has ears, let him hear."* (Mt 13:3-9)

We remember this parable well. It was the same seed; it all received the same rain and the same sunlight. But in different soil, the seed gave different fruit; or even no fruit at all. We have meditated on the fact that nowadays there is no shortage of vocations. There are, perhaps, different difficulties today than those which existed in the past and so, some souls who initially received their calling with enthusiasm grow tepid over time and even wither. Our Lord offers a few explanations for it: lack of solid, profound roots (interior life) or suffocation by material comforts or peer pressure.

We talked about the importance of asking Our Lord to make us ready in Chapter 15. Sure enough, we need to ask for good rains, temperatures and sun exposure. We meditated in Chapter 16 on the need for help and advice which we receive in spiritual guidance. But there are many other things which depend exclusively on us. You see, good farmers prepare the soil for the seed: they mark the area with pegs, remove the weeds, skim the turf, prepare new seedbeds, opening furrows and mixing organic matter into the soil... They make it ready for the seed to grow strong and give much fruit.

In spiritual life we follow a similar process. There are weeds (vices) to remove, and many ways of improving the soil (virtues). Remember the story of the boy in the previous chapter. He had a plan. Like a football player. However, having a plan is the easy part. Carrying it out is the real challenge. Meditating on the example of the saints can have a double effect. On one hand, we feel admiration for the way they received the seed and gave so much fruit; but on the other we can get a bit discouraged when we see the massive difference between their *soil* and ours.

We know saints were not born saints. They also had to struggle to remove many defects and acquire their virtues. *'Yes,'* you could think, *'But in my case there is so much to do!'* Sure; just as in all of us. However, do not consider your improvement in virtue and your overcoming defects as the result of a massive conversion, like something you need to wait for until God grants it to you. See it more as a little improvement every day.

British cycling was never great during the 20th century. Since 1908, just one single cycling gold medal had been won by the UK at the Olympic Games. In 110 years, no British cyclist had ever won the Tour de France. In fact, their performance was so underwhelming that one of the top bike manufacturers refused to sell bikes to the British team, fearing that it would hurt sales if other professionals saw the Brits using their gear!

In 2003 Dave Brailsford became the new performance director. He implemented his philosophy called 'aggregation of marginal gains'. *"The whole principle came from the idea that, if you broke down everything you could think of that goes into riding a bike, and then improved it by 1%, you would get a significant increase when you put them all together"* (Dave Brailsford, 2012).

Brailsford and his team began by making small 'predictable' adjustments. They designed more comfortable bike seats and they rubbed alcohol on the tyres to improve their grip. They provided the riders with electrically heated shorts to maintain ideal muscle temperature during the rides and used biofeedback sensors to monitor their workouts. They tested different fabrics in a wind tunnel and changed their racing suits for lighter and more aerodynamic ones.

But they didn't stop there. They continued to find 1 percent improvements in overlooked and unexpected areas: new massage gels to accelerate muscle recovery, better hygienic procedures to avoid infections and colds; they changed the type of pillow and mattress to improve the athletes' sleep, they even painted the inside of the team truck white, to better spot little bits of dust that would normally slip by unnoticed but could affect the performance of the finely tuned bikes. After making hundreds of small accumulated improvements, the results have astounded the world.

Just five years after Brailsford took over, the British Cycling team won a stunning 60 percent of the available gold medals at the 2008 Olympic Games in Beijing. Four years later, at the Olympic Games in London, they set nine Olympic records and seven world records. That same year, Bradley Wiggins became the first Brit to win the Tour de France. The next year, Chris

Froome won the race, and he would go on to win again in 2015, 2016 and 2017, giving the British team five Tour de France victories in six years. During the ten-year period between 2007 to 2017 alone, British cyclists won 178 world championships and 66 Olympic or Paralympic gold medals and captured five Tour de France victories in what is widely regarded as the most successful run in cycling history.

Moving forwards in our spiritual life, preparing our soil, can be seen in terms of 1% wins. If in the examination of conscience at night we can think about a little improvement for the following day, we can accumulate hundreds of them over time. Improving by 1 percent in a virtue or moving away from a defect doesn't seem to be particularly notable but it can be far more meaningful in the long run. In case you are interested in the maths: if you can get 1 percent better each day for one year, you'll end up thirty-seven times better. Conversely, if you get 1% worse each day for one year, you'll decline nearly down to zero.

So, prepare the soil with small wins. A bit more study today, a bit more concentration in prayer, a bit more punctuality, a bit more order, a bit more patience, a bit more fortitude, a bit more humility, a bit more cheerfulness, a bit more charity, a bit more honesty, a bit more generosity, a bit more industriousness, a bit more... Small wins! Each day 1% better.

Mary, my Mother, help me to never get discouraged by my defects and lack of virtue; infuse in me the drive I need to prepare the soil with little improvements, small wins every day. Let's write down today's resolution. Let's begin now!

18

God wants the lot

> *When Simon Peter saw it, he fell down at Jesus' knees, saying, "Go away from me, Lord, for I am a sinful man!" ...Then Jesus said to Simon, "Do not be afraid; from now on you will be catching people." When they had brought their boats to shore, they left everything and followed him (Lk 5:8-11).*

The disciples left everything. They were ready to do it, as we saw earlier; and so they did it. This idea must penetrate the soul of anyone who prays about vocation. Whatever God is asking from you involves your whole life. To carry out your mission in life, God is not asking for just your spare time. He wants your life.

"*You can't have your cake and eat it too,*" we say sometimes. It means that whatever choice we make in life is ruling out many other options. If we are to follow Christ, just as the Apostles did, we will have to leave some boats and nets on the shore. Those boats and nets are different for everyone, but we all have to give up some things to be able to follow Him. There is no costless vocation; there are no sales, no discounts.

Let's ask ourselves about the many things that we are attached to in our lives. Those things that we like to spend time on: our sports, our rest, our games, our study, our timetable, our plans, our Instagram, our Netflix, our novels, our music... and also our material things: our smartphone, our room, our couch, our clothes, our bed... If Jesus were to ask us to leave those 'boats and nets' on the shore, would we be able to 'leave everything and follow Him'? What things would be more difficult to get rid of?

Now, imagine Peter replying to Jesus, '*O.K. Fine, Lord, I would love to come with you. But couldn't we just do everything in a way that won't interfere with the plans I already have in place right now?*' Or imagine Andrew saying, '*What are the exact working hours you expect from me?*' Or try to picture the young Apostle John asking Jesus, '*At what time am I released on Fridays?*' It would be absurd to find James questioning about his *'holidays'* since all his days with Jesus were *holy* days.

With God's Grace, they were able to drop their nets in their boats and leave everything on the shore. You see? God doesn't offer a set of different plans and then His disciples choose the one that suits them best. God proposes His plan to them and all they have to say is 'Yes' or 'No'. There is no negotiation about the terms and conditions, no 'cookies' that we can accept or reject, no bespoke tailoring, no adaptations...

If, when thinking about any vocation, the first thing that comes to mind is what we would have to give up or cut down or get rid of, then there might be a lot of things between us and our vocation. Precisely, those things that popped into your mind first are the first issues you need to tackle.

St Josemaría tells the story mentioned earlier of a young person whose reaction was to make some mental calculations when he was asked about committing his life: "*If I did, I could do that... I would have to do this other thing...*" The Founder of Opus Dei explains the blunt reply the lad got: "*Here, we don't bargain with the Lord... the invitation of the Lord is something you either take or leave, just as it is. You need to make up your mind: go forward, fully decided and without holding back; otherwise, go away."*

In his *'Screwtape Letters'*, C. S. Lewis writes the letters of an experienced devil to his nephew, an amateurish evil spirit. At one point, he describes with clarity the temptation that drives a soul to try to bargain with God, about not 'overdoing it': "*Talk to him about 'moderation in all things',*" explains the expert devil to his nephew. "*If you can once get him to the point of thinking that 'religion is all very well up to a point', you can feel quite happy about his soul. A moderated religion is as good for us as no religion at all - and more amusing.*"

St Thomas Becket was Archdeacon of Canterbury, appointed as Lord Chancellor by King Henry II. The king could count on him for anything he needed. For this reason, the monarch appointed him Archbishop of Canterbury in 1162. Despite this, he was not a great model of virtue. But after the archdeacon was ordained a priest and then, on the following day consecrated as bishop, something happened to him. Somehow grace brought about a transformation in Becket.

He realised that a bishop was not an appointment, but a vocation. To become a bishop meant becoming a saint - as a bishop. He understood perfectly well that he had not been fulfilling his vocation as a deacon and then felt the urge to be what he was meant to be. A vocation can't be played down. That conversion didn't suit the purposes of the king and eventually St Thomas Becket was killed by Henry II's knights.

There is no easy way to get to Heaven, no shortcuts, no bypass, no effort-saving alternative. Online you can find easy ways to fix things, learn things, get things... but there is no easy route to Heaven. As Peter Kreeft said, "*It's too bad there isn't an easier way, because becoming a saint is not the easiest thing in the world. It's much easier to become an apologist or a philosopher or a theologian."*

So, let's not waste time thinking about how we can reduce our commitment to God as if we were prisoners trying to reduce our sentence. All God wants is our happiness; and our vocation is our way to happiness. Vocation can't be cut into bite-sized chunks. It isn't a salad: we can't just pick some parts and set aside what we don't like.

Let's be honest. Let's make up our mind. Let's decide whether we want to say 'Yes' or 'No', even before God reveals His Will. If we feel weak and indecisive, then let's go to Our Lady: Holy Mary, Star of the Sea, shed some light; St Joseph, my father and lord, don't allow me to try to negotiate terms. My Guardian Angel, make sure I give myself entirely, to the full.

19

God will change your plans

> *Jesus saw two boats by the lake; but the fishermen had gone out of them and were washing their nets. Getting into one of the boats, which was Simon's, he asked him to put out a little from the land. And he sat down and taught the people from the boat. And when he had ceased speaking, he said to Simon, "Put out into the deep and let down your nets for a catch." And Simon answered, "Master, we toiled all night and took nothing! But at your word I will let down the nets." And when they had done this, they enclosed a great shoal of fish; and as their nets were breaking…* (Lk 5:2-6).

Peter and his companions had spent the night fishing. After a long night of toil, all these fishermen wanted was to go home, have some breakfast and take a good nap. But Jesus got into his boat. We can imagine Peter's face when he saw a rabbi in his boat asking him to move it away from the shore to preach from it. *'Why my boat?'* Peter could have thought. *'Why don't you preach from the shore? Or from someone else's boat?'*

But Peter was a good man and Jesus an impressive rabbi, so he released the ties and kept the boat a little way from the crowd. Jesus started preaching. He taught for a while. Peter was tired after the night shift but still listened with attention.

At last Jesus dismissed the crowds. Peter thought it was time to go home but Jesus had another request. The first request was a favour for the people He had to teach. This second request was different. Peter thought Jesus was asking for another favour; instead, Jesus was going to do *him* a favour, as compensation for the troubles and a lesson in faith which his disciples could never forget.

So, for a second time Jesus changed Peter's plans. He asked him to cast off and try fishing again. Maybe a bit reluctant, but still impressed by Jesus, Peter decided to do as he was advised. And then the miracle happened. Let's note three points about the miracle: 1) Peter had to change his plans; 2) If he didn't, he wouldn't have caught the best catch of his life; 3) Peter thought he was doing Jesus a favour - until he discovered it was Jesus who was doing a favour for him.

That's very often the case when God changes our plans. After following his vocation to the priesthood, Joseph Ratzinger had chosen a life of study, research and teaching. He was professor of theology at the Universities of Bonn and Münster and later on in the University of Tübingen. He liked that lifestyle.

But God had other plans. The first turn in his life happened in 1977 when he was appointed archbishop of Munich and Freising. He had to leave his work as a university professor and move to the bishop's palace as pastor of his diocese. After that turnaround, another one came in 1981 when St John Paul II called him to Rome to preside over the Congregation for the Doctrine of the Faith. He could have refused or resisted the burdens he had to carry on his shoulders, the responsibilities that prevented him from doing what he loved - but he obediently accepted.

When he turned 70 years old, he presented Pope St John Paul II with his resignation. He wanted to go back to his homeland and spend his last days, as he put it, "*dedicated to the study and research of some interesting documents and works*" which he had carefully collected over the years. St John Paul II didn't accept his resignation and asked him to remain in his post. When, in April 2005, the Polish Pope died, Cardinal Ratzinger assumed his time for resting had finally arrived. However, God had something else in mind.

Pope Benedict himself explains what happened during his election: "*As the trend in the ballots slowly made me realize that - in a manner of speaking the guillotine would fall on me - I started to feel quite dizzy. I thought that I had done my life's work and could now hope to live out my days in peace. I said to Our Lord with deep conviction, 'Don't do this to me. You have younger and better candidates who could take up this great task with a totally different energy and with different strength.' Evidently, this time He didn't listen to me,*" the Pope said. He kept on explaining how, during the secret deliberations, a fellow cardinal had written him a note, reminding him of the sermon he preached during the funeral Mass for St John Paul II, in which he referred to the biblical passage where Jesus asked the Apostle Peter to follow him.

He said, "*My fellow brother wrote me: 'If the Lord should now tell you, "Follow me," then, remember what you preached. Do not refuse. Be obedient'... This touched my heart. The ways of the Lord are not comfortable, but we were not created for comfort, but for greatness, for good. So in the end, all I could say was 'Yes'. I am trusting in God.*"

The Pope concluded: "*The Lord had other plans for me and here I am among you, not as a passionate scholar of ancient texts, but as the pastor called to encourage all the faithful to cooperate for the salvation of the world, each one doing God's will where he places us to work,*" you and I in the place where God puts us.

Joseph Ratzinger's studies were his boat and nets. From there he could do a great deal of good for many people. But God is not content with us doing 'a great deal of good'. God knows the maximum good that we can do in our lives, with our talents, in our situation. God knew what Joseph Aloisius Ratzinger could do for the world and it wasn't playing the piano in a cottage in his homeland... Pope Benedict left his plans, his studies and lectures (his boats and nets) and said 'Yes' to God. And we are very grateful to him for becoming the instrument God wanted – at the expense of his personal plans.

What Joseph Ratzinger has allowed God to do with his life is amazing! But he could have put his foot down any time he wanted. He could have said 'No' to becoming a priest, or a bishop, or a prefect, or a pope...

Now... what about you? Will the world be grateful to you for allowing God to work marvellous things using you as His instrument?

Mary, my Mother, help me to be ready to change my plans. St Joseph, my father and lord, may I imitate your example to follow God's promptings without delay. My Guardian Angel, don't let me hold back God's schedule.

20

Resignation?

> *"A man had two sons; and he went to the first and said, 'Son, go and work in the vineyard today.' And he answered, 'I will not'; but afterward he repented and went. And he went to the second and said the same; and he answered, 'I will go, sir,' but did not go"* (Mt 21:28-30).

This father had a problem with both his sons. It is clear that they were not very enthusiastic about fulfilling their father's will. The second one seems to understand that obeying his dad was the right thing to do and he, apparently, wanted to do it. But perhaps later he felt a bit lazy, or procrastinated or changed his mind, or all of the above. In the end, he just didn't do it.

The first son, however, was more direct. At the beginning he just didn't want to do it. But later he probably thought about his father and, maybe just out of pity, or even love, he did what he was asked. It is clear, however, that working in the vineyard wasn't really his cup of tea.

Some people have this problem when thinking about their divine calling. Their train of thought could be something like: 'OK. God wants me to be ………. . I wouldn't ever choose that option for me, but since it is God who asks for it, I have no other choice but to resign myself to His Will and do what He says.' It sounds like an actor who has to read a script he didn't write, a script he doesn't even like, but he has to do it because he needs the income. It just seems wrong.

How genuine would it be to 'resign' ourselves to our 'fate' following God's Will?

Let this be clear in our mind: Our vocation is not a duty. It is a privilege!

If we feel like we 'have to' accept it, we haven't understood it correctly. God doesn't choose people to test them, but to bless them. God is not a boss; He is not an employer, a manager, a politician... Read the opening parable again from the beginning. It is about a father asking his children to work in 'their' vineyard. The father doesn't say, '*You*, go and work in *my* vineyard'. He says, "*Son*," (you are my son and I am your father) "*go and work in the vineyard today...*", '*our* family business, *our* vineyard.'

God is not our boss and we are not slaves. We are children. And to make us His children, He had to die on the Cross and shed all His Blood. God is not giving us instructions, orders, commands. God is asking us just as a father asks his child. He is not asking us to work 'for Him.' The salvation of souls is more of a family business. He is working with us in the same vineyard. And to work side by side with God Himself for the salvation of souls is a privilege and not a duty.

As St Josemaría put it, "*Resignation is not a generous word.*" The word 'resignation' often accompanies the word 'fate'. That is absolutely opposed to the freedom of the children of God. It is just not right. If a football player is called to play in the national team, do you think he will accept the offer with 'resignation'? If your local supermarket presented you with a cheque for £1,000, would you accept it with 'resignation'? If your essay was selected for first prize in a competition, would you have to resign yourself to your fate?

Imagine that on a trip to Rome you see the Pope passing by in his pope-mobile. He fixes his eyes on you and, all of a sudden, he asks the driver to stop the car. The pope steps out and comes to you, smiling. Then he invites you to get in the pope-mobile and there he explains to you that he needs someone like you to help him in the Vatican. You think, 'Why me?' And the pope quotes what you have on your CV. He needs someone who speaks the languages you speak, who has studied the subjects you have studied, who has the contacts you have, your skills... Wow! He really knows you. He is not improvising. He expected to meet you there. Now, he expects your answer. Would you 'resign yourself to your fate'?

Vocation is not a duty; it is not a punishment; it is not a random choice from Heaven; it is not an assignment; it is not a liability; it is not a charge; it is not a burden; it is not even an obligation. Vocation is a privilege. The privilege of working side by side with God and helping Him work miracles.

Do you remember the multiplication of the loaves and fish? When Jesus asked His disciples to feed the crowd, Philip made the point that they had nothing to give away. Andrew then added that there was a boy *"with five small barley loaves and two small fish, but how far will they go among so many?"* (Jn 6:9). But the boy gave all of his food to Jesus and Our Lord could feed about 5,000 people. How do you think the boy felt after that? How do you think he felt when he met Jesus after the miracle and Our Lord smiled at him and stroked his hair saying, *'See what* **we** *did with your loaves and fish'*?

That boy felt privileged. The Apostles too, who had seen what the lad did, would smile at him and even tousle his hair jokingly: *'Those were the best fish sandwiches I've ever had!'*

Saints have felt that privilege in their calling. It is not exempt from suffering or toil; but true joy is never free of charge.

Vocation is a mission, a divine calling; our vocation means we are the best choice for a mission; God has selected us; He has appointed us; He has equipped us; He has set up a mission that only we can fulfil. From among billions, God has chosen us. For this divine selection our vocation is not a duty; it is a privilege.

Mary, my Mother and my Queen, help me understand well the privilege of having God's eyes set on me. St Joseph, my father and lord, write with permanent ink upon my heart that God doesn't want slaves, servants or employees. God only wants children who freely want to help Him save souls. My Guardian Angel, it is also an honour to have you with me all the time to work for souls, with God.

21

Simon of Cyrene

> *And when they had mocked him, they stripped him of the purple cloak, and put his own clothes on him. And they led him out to crucify him. And they compelled a passer-by, Simon of Cyrene, who was coming in from the country, the father of Alexander and Rufus, to carry his cross. And they brought him to the place called Golgotha* (Mk 15:20-22).

Simon of Cyrene had no other plans than to get home and have lunch. But he met Jesus on His way to Calvary and the soldiers compelled him to carry the Cross of Our Lord. Few people named in the Gospel have been more envied than Simon of Cyrene by Christians of all times. How many of us would have applied for the honour of carrying the Cross with Jesus! But it was not granted to St John, Our Lady or St Peter... it was granted to the one appointed before all ages, a farmer from Cyrene who had not volunteered.

Mark calls him "*the father of Alexander and Rufus*" without further explanation, taking it for granted that his readers knew who Rufus and Alexander were because they were part of the Christian community. Thus, many understand that Simon himself became a disciple of Our Lord.

But this wasn't his intention on that afternoon of Good Friday.

The Gospel texts that mention him specify that he was forced: "*they compelled this man,*" says St Matthew (27:32); "*they laid the cross on him, and made him carry it behind Jesus,*" describes St Luke (23:26). In any case, it is clear that he didn't volunteer. He probably protested, '*This isn't my cross*', '*I have committed no crime*', '*Why me and not someone else?*' The Convict's appearance was repulsive: wounds bleeding from every inch of His skin, His clothes stained with Blood and dirt, His eyes swollen underneath the horrible Crown of Thorns piercing His scalp... As Isaiah described Him eight centuries before: "*From the sole of the foot even to the head, there is no soundness in it, but bruises and sores and bleeding wounds; they are not pressed out, or bound up, or softened with oil*" (Is 1:6).

Simon of Cyrene had no desire to carry the Cross of that Man. But he was forced. As he took the cross on his shoulders and took his first steps, he couldn't hide his repugnance. The maddening crowd with their yelling and pushing and pulling added more aversion to his task. But he had no choice. So, resigned to his fate, he looked at the summit and kept walking.

However, we can well imagine that as the time passed and he rubbed up against the clothes of Jesus and touched His Wounds and heard His rasping breath, he perceived that there was something special about this Criminal. At some point maybe he saw the Man needed more help and Simon took more of the weight on his back. Perhaps he even remembered having heard about Him in the past, and about His miracles. He didn't seem like a criminal to Simon. What if this Man was innocent as well... like him? Or even more?!

Then he saw the Mother of the Convict and a light illuminated his heart. There was too much suffering in there, too much innocent suffering - and he couldn't understand it. But he had the power to lessen, in some way, the sufferings of this Man and His Mother. And so he did. He started lifting the Cross higher, helping Jesus, encouraging Him, comforting Him, relieving Him, supporting Him... carrying Him.

Simon couldn't remember in what precise moment he forgot he had been compelled to carry the Cross, in what exact instant the Cross started lightening and his eyes started gazing at the Man with love. When many years later he told the story to the disciples who drank from his very words, he couldn't tell at what specific point of the hillside he stopped considering it a duty and started to grasp the honour of his position, the privilege of his mission. It took him years to understand it.

When they reached the summit and he was dismissed, he felt like kissing the Criminal. He had come to feel affection for that Man in the end. He didn't dare to kiss Him, but when he walked away, still looking back at the Man who was going to be crucified, he ran into His Mother. He was startled, still thinking about the Man he had helped to carry the Cross. In his confusion, it took him a second to understand what was going on: the Mother took his hand and kissed it. She smiled at him and said 'Thank you'. He didn't hear her voice but read her lips.

Simon of Cyrene walked back home, engrossed in his thoughts, with a blank stare and clumsy steps after the effort, meditating on what had just happened.

It took him years to understand the privilege of his mission. He saw it in the eyes of Mary, the Mother of Jesus, in the eyes of every Christian he met, everyone who knew what he had done. He couldn't remember the precise moment of his life when he understood that God wanted to meet him on that slope to Calvary, that precise moment on the afternoon of Good Friday, and that God counted on him. The soldiers placed the Cross on his shoulders, but it was Jesus who asked Simon to carry It with Him.

Many times our vocation lacks any 'romantic' feeling of self-fulfilment and realization of the importance of our mission. At times, our vocation is not even attractive at the beginning. We may even feel a bit of aversion to it. But if that is the mission that God has thought up for us, if we are faithful and decide to start carrying it out, the time will come when the 'penny' drops, when we will understand why we, and not someone else, have been entrusted with that task.

In time, something that we may have accepted as a 'duty' will become a passion. If we are faithful, if we say 'Yes', if we start moving forward, we will find that what was a heavy burden at the beginning, has become light - *"For my yoke is easy, and my burden is light"* (Mt 11:30); we will find that what didn't make sense at the beginning, makes sense now - *"What I am doing you do not know now, but afterward you will understand"* (Jn 13:7); we will find ourselves walking with Jesus even if we couldn't see Him for a while - *"While they were talking and discussing, Jesus himself came near and went with them"* (Lk 24:15).

One day we will discover that, like Simon of Cyrene, we have the power to lessen the sufferings of Jesus and His Mother, to help Him, comfort Him, support Him, carry Him... to many souls. One day, if we accept our calling, we will find Our Lady smiling at us as well; she will take our hand, and kiss us, and 'Thank' us, and keep us with her in the place reserved for those who had the privilege to help her Son co-redeem the world.

22

The freedom of the children of God

> *But the serpent said to the woman, "You will not die. For God knows that when you eat of it your eyes will be opened, and you will be like God, knowing good and evil." So...she took of its fruit and ate; and she also gave some to her husband, and he ate. Then the eyes of both were opened, and they knew that they were naked* (Gen 3:4-7).

We were created free. Somehow, our first parents felt the presence of God as a threat, a limitation to their freedom. They wanted to get rid of their dependence on God. As we know, it had the opposite effect. They became slaves of their passions. However, God would not allow this state of affairs to remain, and decided to pay our ransom and set us free again. The ransom was expensive: it cost all the Blood of Christ. But God thought it was still a bargain; that's how much He values our freedom.

The Creator made it clear: He doesn't want dutiful servants. He wants loving children. But men are still suspicious. We still think that the one Who paid so dearly for our freedom prefers that we don't use it. And we are afraid to allow Him to come into our lives.

For people who feel the demands of God as a threat, a limitation to their freedom, Pope Benedict said, "*Are we not perhaps all afraid in some way? If we let Christ enter fully into our lives, if we open ourselves totally to him, are we not afraid that He might take something away from us? Are we not perhaps afraid to give up something significant, something unique, something that makes life so beautiful? Do we not then risk ending up diminished and deprived of our freedom?... No! If we let Christ into our lives, we lose nothing, nothing, absolutely nothing of what makes life free, beautiful and great. No! Only in this friendship are the doors of life opened wide. Only in this friendship is the great potential of human existence truly revealed. Only in this friendship do we experience beauty and liberation. And so, today, with great strength and great conviction, on the basis of long personal experience of life, I say to you, dear young people: Do not be afraid of Christ! He takes nothing away, and he gives you everything. When we give ourselves to him, we receive a hundredfold in return. Yes, open, open wide the doors to Christ – and you will find true life.*"

They say that one day a sister of St Thomas Aquinas asked him, "*Brother, what is necessary to become a saint?*" The wise man, a man of few and precise words, replied, "*Will it.*"

It is as simple as that. At the end of the day it is a matter of will. If you want it, then you won't lack God's grace. No matter how difficult it might seem to you, you are always free to say 'Yes' or 'No'. As we considered before, a servant has no choice when asked something by a master. But children are free to comply or deny when asked by their father.

In the passage of the rich young man, the man asked Jesus about what was needed to inherit Eternal Life. When Jesus quoted the list of the Commandments, the youngster said that he had been fulfilling those and asked what 'else' was needed. Our Lord's reply is the point we are trying to consider here. In the Latin text, Jesus said to him, "*Si vis perfectus esse...*" The translation is easy: "*If you want to be perfect, then...*"

"*If you want...*" - as if saying, '*If you choose to be perfect... because this is entirely up to you. You can choose otherwise...*'

We can't ever talk too much about freedom. It is the essence of this whole book. Vocation is a choice. God chooses us freely. We choose to follow Him freely. Two wills, God's and ours, meet and then make the miracle happen.

God doesn't force His children. But it helps to consider Him as a Father in need. A Father Who can't do some things without the help of His children. A loving Father who doesn't impose Himself; a Father begging for help.

God, Omnipotent... and begging? Yes. That's it.

If we could say that God **forces** His children into anything, it is into making use of their freedom. This must always be fresh in our mind: after the Death of Christ on the Cross, we have *an obligation to be free*. Freedom has become a gift that we are not just entitled to use; we are coerced into effecting it.

Without freedom there is no love - and that is all God is asking from us, for our love for Him to correspond to His Love for us. Exactly as St Thomas taught, all it takes to love is to *will it*.

Vocation is all about freedom. Do you remember the film 'The Matrix'? Morpheus shows Neo what the Matrix is and how his existence has been a life of slavery even if he didn't notice. Then he gives Neo the choice to choose freely. To be liberated he must want to be. "*There's a difference between knowing the path and walking the path,*" says Morpheus. So, once the path has been laid before the main character, a personal decision has to be made. *"I'm trying to free your mind, Neo,"* Morpheus explains. *"But I can only show you the door. You're the one that has to walk through it."* This is true of your vocation as well. God can reveal it to you, but He won't push you through.

That's the secret of our vocation and the secret of holiness. St Peter didn't have to say 'Yes'. He could have remained a fisherman on the lake of Galilee. St Paul could have ignored the Voice that met him on his way to Damascus, St Mark could have stayed at home instead of accompanying his cousin St Barnabas and St Paul on their evangelical trips. St Augustine could have ended his life as he started it. St Thomas More could have taken the oath that Henry VIII demanded and stayed alive. St John of God could have ignored the urge to repent and change that struck him while listening to a homily of St John of Avila and could have continued living his sinful life. Bl John Henry Newman could have resisted the inclination to convert and complicate his life and that of his relatives. St John Paul II could have disregarded his call to the priesthood... They were all free to choose. They didn't **have to** do what God wanted, but we remember them because they **wanted to** do it.

The conclusion of these paragraphs is simple. In computing terms, we could try to do a *search* on your life (control + F) to find all the instances of '*have to*' in your prayer and then *replace* them with '*want to.*'

Our Lady, Mother of Good Counsel, help me to use my freedom as God wants. St Joseph, my father and lord, help me to feel free. My Guardian Angel, don't let me be a slave to anyone or anything. Free to love.

23

Let's put love and not duty at the centre

> *"A man had two sons; and he went to the first and said, 'Son, go and work in the vineyard today.' And he answered, 'I will not'; but afterward he repented and went. And he went to the second and said the same; and he answered, 'I go, sir,' but did not go"* (Mt 21:28-30).

We don't know much about the first son. We don't know if he was lazy, if he was tired, if he was feeling unwell… but later on he recovered and decided to do what his father had asked of him. Maybe the opposite happened to his brother. After accepting the request maybe he felt sick or had another problem.

There is much that we don't know. However, there is one thing that we can guess: these two children didn't love their dad much. Because if they had loved their dad, one wouldn't have said 'No' to him and the other would have fulfilled his promise.

We know that, after saying 'No', the first son had second thoughts: he *repented*, we are told, and went. But what kind of second thought did he have? Maybe he felt sorry for his dad. Maybe he thought about the family business and his inheritance and thought it prudent to comply. Maybe he remembered that the vineyard was his and his personal profit depended on it. Maybe he later found himself at a loose end and decided to do something...

You see? There could be many reasons for him to repent; some of them nobler than others. But if we think about the most noble of them all, we know that it should be love.

We would like to think that, when he saw his father leaving the room, he understood how unfair his reply had been. It came to mind how much his father loved him. He remembered how much the old man had done for him. He couldn't stop thinking that his father was a good man and deserved a good son. He pictured his father working hard for years to allow him and his brother to have a good life and to provide for them in the past, in the present and for the future.

Maybe, through the window, he could see his father going alone to the vineyard with the pickaxe on his shoulder and that made him feel bad about his reply. He stood up immediately and went to work in the vineyard. In silence he took his place next to his dad and started digging with his spade. His dad smiled but said nothing.

It was a scorching day, long and exhausting. As he wiped the sweat from his brow and shooed away the flies, he glanced at his dad who was working a few yards away. He knew his father looked at him from time to time. And he smiled as well.

At the end of the day his dad put his arm round his son's shoulder and invited him to go back home. They drank water, they chatted about the vineyard, they laughed and arrived home in time for dinner. By then the father could no longer remember the reply his good son had given him when he first asked him to go to work. All the old man could feel then was the privilege of having such a good son.

And the young chap? Lying down on his mat, exhausted after that long day of work, taking a deep breath and looking up at the stars, resting the back of his head on his palms, couldn't help smiling with satisfaction. His old man was over the moon. He had done what his father wanted him to do and he was elated, overjoyed recalling all he had done for his father, for his family, for his future... But most of all, he was proud of being the son of such a father.

This latter version of the story sounds more gracious than the former possibilities; it just looks right. The son did all that out of love and not out of personal interest.

We never get tired of repeating it: we are children of God. We have been given a great archetype to imitate - Jesus Christ, the Son of God - who has left us an example, so that we should follow in His steps (1 *Pe* 2:21). We need to keep our eyes on Him, to try to be like Him, act like Him, think like Him, behave like Him, love like Him.

Antoni Gaudi is a good example of this imitation of Christ. When he was commissioned the *Sagrada Familia* basilica in 1894, he wanted to prepare himself following the advice of Fra Angelico (1387-1455), the famous painter and friar who said, "*Those who want to paint Christ have to live with Him.*" From that moment he abandoned the pleasures of life, his stylish attire, gourmet tastes and celebrity status. Instead, he became well-known in Barcelona for his austerity and modest dressing. He gave away his salary to pay for the new building and attended daily Mass.

What started off being an assignment, a job, for Gaudi became a passion to which he gave his life. More than a hired architect, he became a son building a house for his Father. In the same way, our vocation is not a duty commissioned to a servant or an employee. It is a task that a Father entrusts to His child.

When praying about vocation let's never forget to address the dialogue properly. It is a conversation of a Father with His child, you and me. Just like in the parable, it's our Father who is asking us to work **with** Him in the vineyard. Pay attention to the preposition: We don't just work **for** Him. We work for souls... **with** Him. We can repeat it again and again: our vocation is not the duty of a servant; it is the privilege of a child of God.

Mary, my Mother, Virgin Most Renowned, by spending hours with your Son, you eventually managed to imitate Him, to take after Him - Mother like Son. Mother, help me to understand the privilege of being a child of such a Father. St Joseph, my father and lord, teach me to do things out of love and not out of duty. My Guardian Angel, remind me often of my condition: being God's child and not God's slave.

24

Mind your own business

> *Jesus said to Peter, "Follow me." Peter turned and saw following them the disciple whom Jesus loved...When Peter saw him, he said to Jesus, "Lord, what about this man?" Jesus said to him, "If it is my will that he remain until I come, what is that to you? Follow me!"* (Jn 21:19-22)

Jesus asked Peter to follow Him. Peter turned and saw John there behind him and wondered if Jesus was asking him to follow them as well. We don't know exactly what was on Peter's mind. What we do know is that Jesus asked him to stop worrying about other people and do what he was told. John, in his turn, would be asked by the Master whatever He wanted from him. Peter, Prince of the Apostles, was not going to be consulted or even informed about God's Will for someone else.

In other words, 'Peter, mind your own business.'

The moment we start comparing ourselves with others, we start losing our peace. Vocation is personal. What God is exacting from you is different from whatever He wants to exact from others. It is a childish argument. You ask a child to clear the table and all he is worried about is what his brother will be asked, whether he has done it before or will do it later, or the perception that it is *'always me!'*

Apart from the fact that you are not anyone else, there is the profound truth of your ignorance about others' situations. *'What is God asking of him?' 'Why me and not her?' 'Why does God want me to do 'this' but wants him to do 'that'?'* This questioning is not just a waste of time: it is a lack of humility, charity and peace.

The following is based on a true story. It was a very dry summer. Patrick (not his real name) was shaving when he gazed out at his neighbours' lawn (the Collins family - again, a fictional name). He was shocked: it was so vividly green that Patrick couldn't help feeling ashamed of his back garden, a yellow dry lawn with patches of bare soil... He made up his mind, there and then, to revive his lawn by watering it daily and giving the plants special plant food as well.

After a week, his grass recovered a bit of life and colour but, peering out of his window every morning, he could see his neighbour's lawn was more luscious than the Yankee Stadium. His sorrow turned to jealousy. (He even thought about pouring some detergent or any other poison on his neighbours' garden but managed to overcome the temptation.) However, he didn't like his back garden anymore. He gave up on it. The Collins' lawn was going to be greener anyway.

Going out one evening to walk his dog Sparky (the dog's name is also concealed) he met Mrs Collins carrying shopping bags from her car to the kitchen. Patrick saw a wonderful opportunity to get into the neighbours' home and have a close-up look at their lawn. He offered to lend Mrs Collins a hand and started taking her bags inside. From the kitchen window he could see the back garden. Mrs Collins discovered him peering through the window. *"What do you think about the lawn?"* she asked. Patrick was prudent to hide his feelings. She invited him to go out and take a closer look.

Patrick hurried out and, bending down, started stroking the blades of grass. Then he had one of the most profound epiphanies of his life. Just as it was dawning on him, he heard Mrs Collins corroborate his new life-changing discovery. It was plastic! *"It was a brilliant idea. It looks so real!"* she said behind him. Apparently, now Brendan (we conceal her husband's name also) didn't have to water or cut it anymore. *"Best choice ever!"* concluded Mrs Collins.

It sounds amusing, but it is very real. Most people feel jealous of friends and colleagues when they see their Instagram and Facebook posts, thinking everyone else seems to have a better life. In this new era of displaying '*fictitious happiness*' and '*photoshopped boasting,*' nothing stands up to scrutiny. But what all these things elicit is the feeling of being miserable and dissatisfied with their own 'back garden' - which was perfectly fine until it was compared to the neighbours'. It looked greener, yes. But it was synthetic.

One of the difficulties that some young people experience nowadays is to feel that everyone else is luckier than they are. Why does God ask me to give myself in this vocation whilst my friends can have an easy and happy life? Get this into your head: '*Easy*' and '*happy*' are mutually exclusive concepts. If life is *easy*, it is not *happy*. If life is *happy*, it is not *easy*. Real happiness is never on boastful display. Genuinely happy people don't need others' 'likes' and approval. A recent study showed that an average of five attempts were needed for every smiling photograph on social media. And almost half of them were 'edited'. That's the synthetic lawn. Real happiness doesn't need 'editing'. A real smile doesn't need those 'attempts.'

God doesn't use social media. You can't edit your life for Him.

When God calls, He doesn't ask for opinions. We need to decide if we want to live our lives as God wants or as others want; if we want to compare ourselves to Christ or to the latest celebrity; if we want to BE happy or just '*look like*' we are happy. "*You don't become a saint by comparing yourself to a sinner*," says Mark Hart.

We can't be like children on Christmas night who, just after opening their presents, start looking around to see what others got and whether those presents were better or worse than their own. They can feel disappointed not by what *they* got (most likely what they asked for) but by what *others* got.

Just as Jesus asked Peter not to worry about John, when He reveals your vocation to you, you don't need to see '*what others got.*' Your vocation is God's gift for you. Remember Patrick growing disappointed with his back garden: check if you are also comparing your lot to the synthetic grass of your neighbour.

There is no easy vocation. All vocations have five stars. All of them demand everything. Holiness will always be heroic for a pilot, a pharmacist or a philosopher; for a priest, a friar, a nun, a father or a mother...

Mary, my Mother, help me to give thanks to God in advance for my vocation and for the vocation of everyone else; intercede for us so that we can fulfil it with generosity, unconcerned about what people think of us.

25

Not all that glitters is gold

> *As Jesus was getting into the boat, the man...begged him that he might be with him. But he refused, and said to him, "Go home to your friends, and tell them how much the Lord has done for you, and how he has had mercy on you." And he went away and began to proclaim in the Decapolis how much Jesus had done for him; and all men marvelled* (Mk 5:18-20).

The man wanted to follow Jesus closely, like the Apostles. Instead, Jesus asked him to go back to his family and proclaim the Gospel there, among his relatives and friends. Does it mean that Jesus didn't want the man to follow Him? No. It means that there are many different ways to fulfil God's Will to perfection and bring souls to Him.

Fear of making mistakes can paralyse souls. That has never been an issue for saints even if they did make mistakes. Because there is something they understood perfectly well: *to make a mistake out of generosity towards God can never be counterproductive.*

It may look like some vocations are better than others. It may look to some people that being called to be a bishop would be better than being called to be a carpenter. This mistake is widespread. It happens all the time when comparing people.

You see? When people start comparing football players they fall into this error. They may start saying that Neymar is better than Thibaut Courtois. Courtois? Who is that guy? He is the Belgium goalkeeper. The point is that if you ask Neymar to guard the goal it is going to be a disaster. Any professional goalkeeper, even in the second or third division, is better than Neymar... in goal. So, who is the best? Well, it depends on the position.

The same happens with vocations. Which vocation is best: to be a priest, a celibate physician, or a teacher, the father of a large family? There is no 'best' in general. It is the best for you or for me or for St Francis... It all depends on what God had in mind for me. That is the best vocation. It is not good to become a priest when God is asking someone to be a father of a large family. But also the opposite is true. There is no second-rate vocation. Every vocation is top. Every single one entails a calling to heroic holiness.

St Benedict Labre happened to have an uncle, a parish priest, who gladly received him and undertook his early education for the priesthood. He showed remarkable devotion to the Eucharist and love for God but, after a while, Benedict's uncle doubted his nephew would ever become a priest. Then Benedict thought he should become a Trappist monk. His uncle and family put him off. By then an epidemic fell upon the city, and uncle and nephew busied themselves in the service of the sick. Among the last victims of the epidemic was the uncle himself. His death left Benedict without a home. He made up his mind again to join a religious Order and explained his determination to his parents. They refused for a while but eventually gave in and Benedict set off with a glad heart in the direction of La Trappe.

He arrived there only to be disappointed. In the abbey, the monks had made a resolution to admit no more people unless they were absolutely sound in body. Benedict did not come up to their requirements. Still he would not surrender. For a time he went to live with another parish priest, a distant relative, so that he might continue his studies and perfect his Latin. If the Trappists would not have him, perhaps the Carthusians would. He went off to ask for admission to the Carthusians of Montreuil. The monks were very kind, as Carthusians always are; they showed him every mark of affection, but they also told him that he had no vocation to their Order.

If one Carthusian monastery would not have him, then perhaps another would. He tramped off to the monastery of Longuenesse and, to his joy, the monks there agreed to give him a trial. But the trial did not last long. He went back home but didn't give up. Since the Carthusians had said that he could not be received among them because he knew no philosophy, he found someone willing to teach him and, as much as he disliked the study, he persevered for the year as he had been told. Then he applied once more at Montreuil. The conditions had been fulfilled, he was now older, his health had improved… and they received him. But the result was again the same. After six weeks of trial the monks had to tell him that he was not made for their religious order - and asked him to leave.

Benedict didn't go home this time; he made up his mind never to go home again. He would try the Trappists once more, or some other confined Order; perhaps he would have to go from monastery to monastery till at last he found peace, but he would persevere. With hope he came to La Trappe and again was disappointed; the good monks declined even to reconsider his case. But he went on to the Abbey of Sept Fonts and there was accepted; for the third time he settled down to test his vocation as a monk. The trial lasted only eight months.

Finally, he understood that God wanted something different from him. St Benedict settled on a life of poverty and pilgrimage. He first travelled to Rome on foot, subsisting on what he could get by begging. He then travelled to most of the major shrines in Europe. His fame became well known and people went to him for advice and prayers. He died in Rome on 16 April 1783, during Holy Week, and was buried in the Church of Santa Maria ai Monti. His reputation for holiness and devotion spread like wildfire in no time. His confessor, Marconi, wrote his biography and attributed 136 separate cures to his intercession within three months of his death.

It may seem like a Trappist or a Carthusian is a better vocation than that of a beggar. St Benedict himself seemed to have been a bit confused about this as well. Yet, the best vocation is always 'our vocation.'

St Thomas More was also a bit perplexed regarding his vocation. For a period of four years he tried to live like a Carthusian monk in a monastery. There he was persuaded that the Carthusians' austerity was not for him. Then he entered a Franciscan convent in Greenwich. After a while it was clear to the Friars there that he did not have their vocation. Eventually, he understood that what God needed from him was to sanctify himself in the middle of the world. His life was in no way less demanding than that of the religious orders, as his martyrdom proved. His vocation was still a call to perfection, heroic holiness, one hundred per cent sanctity, but different from the Carthusians or the Franciscans.

St Camillus of Lellis entered the novitiate as a Capuchin friar. But eventually he wasn't admitted to the Order. He kept searching for his vocation until he understood that God was asking something else of him, no less exacting than the Capuchin life: becoming the founder of an institution to care for the sick.

Following her husband's death and with her children fully grown-up, St Jeanne De Lestonnac, at the age of 46 turned to a contemplative life and entered the Cistercian Monastery in Toulouse. She found great peace and satisfaction in the monastic life, but, after six months, she became very ill and had to leave the monastery. After a few years trying to find out what God wanted from her, she became the founder of a new teaching order for young women.

All these saints have something in common. They didn't understand their vocation well at the beginning. But they didn't lack generosity as you can see. They gave themselves entirely to the plan they thought was God's Will, even if it wasn't. Do you think God could get upset to see these men and women making a mistake out of love and with full generosity? Certainly not!

Fear of making mistakes shouldn't paralyse us. It is clear that all of them had a time of reflection and trial during which they could see if that was really God's Will for them or not. They trusted God and ended up becoming saints, even if it took them a while to fully understand God's Will.

When thinking about your vocation, remember that an 'excess' of generosity and trust is never a mistake. God doesn't abandon those who abandon themselves to Him. Generosity is always rewarded.

Mary, Mother of Good Counsel, help me to be generous with God; don't allow me to be afraid of making mistakes if I am trying to give God what I think He is asking of me. May I trust Him completely, just as you did.

26

Prayer

> *In the sixth month the angel Gabriel was sent from God to a city of Galilee named Nazareth, to a virgin betrothed to a man whose name was Joseph, of the house of David; and the virgin's name was Mary. And he came to her and said, "Hail, full of grace, the Lord is with you!"* (Lk 2:26-28)

Traditional representations of the Annunciation usually portray the Angel finding Mary immersed in prayer with the Scriptures in her hands. During Our Lady's prayer the Archangel Gabriel delivered her mission to her. A couple of times St Luke tells us that *"Mary kept all these things, pondering them in her heart"* (Lk 2:19,51).

She meditated on everything that concerned Jesus – what was said about Him, what happened to Him, His Words, His Actions, things that were written in the Scripture about Him, what the Angel said... Mothers have this ability to remember everything concerning their children. But we are told not only that Mary remembered them, but that she 'pondered' them. *Ponder* comes from the Latin to weigh something, to judge the worth of something. The dictionary defines *ponder* as 'to consider something deeply, thoughtfully, and thoroughly'. That's what Mary did with everything that concerned Jesus.

That *consideration* is meditation; it happens in prayer, in our conversation with God. If you want to know your friend's opinion about something, you need to talk to your friend. You ask and your friend replies – and that triggers a dialogue. Likewise, if you want to know what God thinks about your vocation, you'd better talk to Him about it. If we don't speak to Him, how is He supposed to give us an answer?

We talk to God in prayer. God talks to us in prayer. St Teresa of Avila described prayer as "*being on terms of friendship with God frequently conversing in secret with Him who, we know, loves us*" (*Life* 8, 5). Everyone who wants to know his or her vocation has to be determined to become a soul of prayer. To spend time conversing with God, getting acquainted with His Words, His Life, His Deeds... spending time like friends do: talking about what they want to talk about.

Some people want to know what their vocation is but they don't pray. It is impossible to find our vocation if we are inconsistent in that friendship with God, if we don't talk to Him, or do it sporadically (only when we find it easy, when we feel like praying). We say that friends are loyal if we can count on them, anytime, through thick and thin. If a person only wants to help us when she feels like helping, or only replies to our calls when she has nothing else to do, or is only available for us when she finds herself at a loose end, then she is not a loyal friend. God wants to talk to us every day, not just when we feel like praying.

With friends there is confidence. We can talk about football or school things, or we can touch on personal matters, with the intimacy that mutual trust radiates. But beware: reflection is not prayer. In fact, the word reflection originates from the Latin word '*reflexionem*', a combination of '*re*' and '*flex*', which means 'to bend or fold' in order to see ourselves, as if to see our reflection in the mirror. Reflecting is important, but it is not a conversation with God.

To be silent in front of the tabernacle is a big step, but it is not prayer yet; to just think about a spiritual topic or about God is not prayer; mere introspection and reflection on our own behaviour is not prayer; a monologue is not prayer. Prayer is not a silent time to organise our day, to prepare a conversation or to read spiritual books. Prayer is a conversation with God and nothing else.

"We all know that prayer is to talk with God," teaches St Josemaría. *"But someone may ask, 'What should I talk about?' What else could you talk about but his interests and the things that fill your day? About the birth of Jesus, his years among us, his hidden life, his preaching, his miracles, his redemptive passion and death, his resurrection. And in the presence of the Triune God, invoking Mary as our mediatrix and beseeching St Joseph, our father and lord, to be our advocate, we will speak of our everyday work, of our family, of our friendships, of our big plans and little shortcomings."*

And in another text he explains what we should talk about in our prayer with God: *"About Him, about yourself: joys, sorrows, successes and failures, noble ambitions, daily worries, weaknesses! And acts of thanksgiving and petitions: and Love and reparation."* It is, in the end, what St Teresa told us: an intimate conversation between friends. And the result of it is *"to get to know him and to get to know yourself: 'to get acquainted!'"* (St Josemaría).

In the intimacy of that conversation with God we can, indeed, reflect on what happens in our lives. But we don't just think about it, as someone who talks to himself; we talk to Our Lord about it. Those desires for holiness that have been bubbling up in our heart lately; the craving to do great things with our lives, that longing for meaning; the aspiration to make an impact in the lives of others; the uneasiness of ignoring what God is expecting from us; our hunger for happiness, our thirst for love, our inclination to greatness, our dreams, our passions, our projects and plans... All that is the topic of our conversation with the One Who Loves us more than we can fathom.

What was Mary talking to God about when the Archangel came to deliver God's message during her prayer? We don't know. All we can tell is that God loved that prayer, for He loved Mary and Mary loved Him. Let's consider this: Jesus loves to talk to me as much as He loved to chat with St John or St Peter or St Mary Magdalene.

Let's ask Our Lady, Teacher of Prayer, to help us understand how everything changes inside and out, when we decide to have a daily conversation with our Father God, who loves us so much... How much God loves my prayer!

27

God has put people there to help you

> *As Saul journeyed he approached Damascus, and suddenly a light from heaven flashed about him. And he fell to the ground and heard a voice saying to him, "Saul, Saul, why do you persecute me?" And he said, "Who are you, Lord?" And he said, "I am Jesus, whom you are persecuting; but rise and enter the city, and you will be told what you are to do"* (Acts 9:3-6).

We are familiar with the conversion of St Paul. That day, on his way to Damascus, God changed the course of his life. A day he never forgot. Many years later he was still repeating the story: "*As I made my journey and drew near to Damascus, about noon a great light from heaven suddenly shone about me...*" (*Acts* 22:6). With precision, St Paul says a long time later that it all happened "*at midday*" (*Acts* 26:13).

But there is something remarkable in that encounter. Jesus explains to Saul that he is fighting on the wrong team; that he is wasting his life and talents. When St Paul realises he has to take a U-turn, he asks Jesus, "*What shall I do, Lord?*" (*Acts* 22:10). And here comes the 'unexpected' part of the conversation.

Instead of giving Saul precise instructions about what he must do for the rest of his life, Jesus says to him, "*Rise, and go into Damascus, and there you will be told all that is appointed for you to do.*" There in Damascus, Our Lord had prepared a man, Ananias by name, to tell Paul what God expected him to do. Do you see the point?

We can imagine St Paul being a bit confused, arguing with Jesus: '*But, Lord, if You are already here... why don't You explain to me what I must do? Why would You send me to someone else? I am in front of You right now; what need is there to have another interlocutor? Who is this Ananias, anyway?*'

It would be a fair argument, would it not? If God wants to deliver His message to St Paul, to send him to spread Christianity, to preach the Gospel to the Gentiles, to make him reach as far as Rome and the ends of the known world in his evangelical journeys... why does He need a mediator? Surely, whatever Ananias had to do, God could do it better! But remember that even if we don't understand them, God's plans are always the best ones. Our Lord could say with the Backstreet Boys that '*I want it that way.*' Full stop. End of story.

Therefore, God counts on the help of other people to direct souls towards their vocation. If people ask for advice to buy a new smartphone, to download a new app, to choose a university or to read a new book, is it not sensible to ask for advice when making the most important decisions of our lives? Our vocation is personal, of course, but consulting someone who can understand, someone who has the wisdom, knowledge and prudence to help in these matters is also part of God's plan.

We lose no freedom when asking questions of someone who can guide us. Quite the contrary: the more we know about the different options which lay open before us, the more we know ourselves, our limitations, our talents, the demands of the different vocations, the experience of those who have those vocations and lead their lives following them faithfully... the more we know, the more free we are and the better prepared we are to avoid making a mistake.

In the lives of God's children there is no luck, there is no room for chance. God doesn't take any chances. With His Providence, He prepares our lives. And part of His Providence is to surround us with people who can help us. Nobody has randomly appeared in your life.

Of course, not all opinions are equally valuable. We would not treat our next-door neighbour's opinion about a chest infection as equally reliable as the advice of our doctor. We can check the opinion of Internet users about different tablets to treat that infection online. We can even make a poll and take the pill that has been democratically chosen. It still seems more sensible to follow the opinion of the doctor.

God has provided specialists to deal with spiritual matters. And all saints have always had recourse to them as *spiritual guides*. When he was in the seminary, St John Bosco thought about becoming a Franciscan Friar, fearing that otherwise he wouldn't persevere in his priestly vocation. In one of this dreams he heard, "*God has prepared you another harvest.*" He was perplexed until a blacksmith friend of his recommended him to ask Don Cafasso, a priest renowned for his common and supernatural sense. Don Cafasso advised him to continue his studies in the seminary and wait – because Heaven would not deny him the light he needed at its proper time. And sure enough, it happened. St John Bosco became the founder of the Salesians, a religious institute that has served the Church with abundant fruit.

In 1601 Jane Frances of Chantal was widowed. She was 24 and had four children. She started asking God for a holy and wise spiritual director that could guide her. In 1604 she met St Francis de Sales. He was the guide she was looking for. She raised her children and administered her fortune attending to the poor and the sick. When her children had grown up and left home, she became a nun and started, with St Francis de Sales, the Order of the Visitation of Holy Mary. When St Francis died, she went to St Vincent de Paul for spiritual advice. We can tell one thing about St Jane Frances of Chantal: she knew how to choose a spiritual director.

Let us ask Our Lord, through the intercession of the Blessed Virgin Mary, that just as she had Gabriel, St Paul had Ananias, St Bosco had Don Cafasso and St Jane had St Francis and St Vincent, so we too may find the guide we need to see better what God plans for each of us.

28

Do I have to do what I am told?

> *Now when Jesus was born in Bethlehem of Judea in the days of Herod the king, behold, wise men from the East came to Jerusalem, saying, "Where is he who has been born king of the Jews? For we have seen his star in the East, and have come to worship him"* (Mt 2:1-2).

You remember the story well. These Wise Men came from the other side of the world to follow a star. They had a pretty clear idea of where they should go: to the West. They didn't know the exact coordinates but they didn't stop walking across the desert. They were sure that, once in the area, they could ask and find the Person they were looking for.

In a certain primary school the little ones were putting on a Christmas play. At the proper time, the three children who were playing the roles of the Wise Men started deliberating over who they should ask for directions. Finally, one of them concluded, "*Let's ask King Herod, he will tell us where to go.*" Suddenly, a little girl from the audience started shouting at them rather hysterically, "*NO! Herod is evil. Don't go to him! He wants to kill the Baby!*" Everybody laughed; but, to the frustration of the 'little spoiler', the Wise Men didn't change the script of the play.

The girl had a point. Of all the people the Wise Men could ask, they went to the one with the fewest recommendations. However, it was precisely Herod who put them on the right path. For God can use any instrument He wants – including an 'evil' one.

Like the Wise Men, we also have to ask (as we considered in the previous chapter) but also like them, we should remember that God can use instruments of *His* liking which may not be to *everybody's liking*.

'If the people you ask for advice have their own vocation,' you could ask, *'would they not try to pull the wool over my eyes?'* As if when you ask a priest about vocation he would probably try to sell *'his own brand.'* If you ask a Friar, then he will try to coax you into entering his monastery; or a nun, her convent...

This is not how it works. Anyone who gives advice on the spiritual life knows they are accountable to God. A spiritual director is not running a family business. Happiness, holiness and the salvation of souls are at stake here. In that sense, there is no other interest, no other agenda than to help souls find their vocation and support them in following it.

Besides, nobody wants to admit into his or her institution someone who hasn't got a vocation for it. Many holy founders were clear on this message. St Joseph of Calasanz repeated several times: "*Don't be afraid to open wide a hundred doors to let people out and to close ninety nine to let in those who want to join us.*" St Josemaría put it in similar terms: "*The door is always open to leave. But to get in, you will have to push hard.*" They follow the same doctrine of St Paul. When giving advice to Timothy about discerning vocations for the priesthood, he writes: "*Do not be hasty in the laying on of hands, nor participate in another man's sins; keep yourself pure*" (1 Tim 5:22).

In any case, we don't have to be very shrewd to know when someone is trying to manipulate us. But the fact that someone has a vocation shouldn't make us suspicious that they are trying to lure us down their same path. In fact, when we start realising that our path could be a particular one, it would be imprudent not to ask someone who has been treading that path for years.

The first person to discover our vocation will be ourselves. Our spiritual guide won't tell us what our vocation is. When we find out, we will tell that person what it is. God will not reveal our vocation to anybody else but ourselves.

A spiritual director is not an oracle. All he or she can do is to pray and give some advice. That person will not sort out our vocational problem. No one has the right to give or assign vocations to anyone else except God Himself.

However, even though spiritual guides can't tell us exactly what our vocation is, they can more accurately define what our vocation is not. They can have a broad picture and see things that we may not be aware of.

We have read before about St Benedict Labre and St Thomas More. The Carthusians told them that they didn't have a vocation for their order. The Carthusians didn't tell them what vocation they *did* have – for they didn't know. All they could tell with greater precision is that they didn't have *that* particular vocation.

By the same token, a religious person couldn't tell us that we HAVE a vocation to their Order – they could make a mistake very easily. But they could tell us with greater certainty that we DON'T have it (if that were the case) because they know what they are talking about.

Going back to the Gospel: Herod himself didn't know where the King of the Jews was, but he knew a bit more than the Wise Men in that regard. He knew the prophecies. He couldn't tell those men the exact coordinates of where Jesus was – he just knew it had to be around Bethlehem. However, Herod could tell the Wise Men with total certainty that Jesus was not in his palace.

Sure enough, Herod (with his evil intentions) can't be put on the same level as a good spiritual director, but the idea still stands: just as Herod was the person consulted for knowing most about the inhabitants of his palace, so we can always receive sound advice from people who may know more about their particular vocation. We can, therefore, finish this chapter answering the question that opens it: '*Do I have to do what I am told?*' No. We don't '*have to*'. But it would be imprudent to disregard that piece of advice if it is sound.

Let's ask Our Lady, Virgin Most Prudent, to inspire spiritual guides to help souls understand God's plans for them, without imposing their views and opinions but just helping them to discern their vocation, supporting them with their prayer and sacrifice and providing prudent advice to help the light of God reach their souls.

29

Trials

> *Being sent out by the Holy Spirit, [Paul and Barnabas] went down to Seleucia, and from there they sailed to Cyprus. When they arrived at Salamis, they proclaimed the word of God in the synagogues of the Jews. And they had John to assist them... Now Paul and his companions set sail from Paphos and came to Perga in Pamphylia. And John left them and returned to Jerusalem (Acts 13:4-5,13).*

The story of this young man is very interesting. His full name is John Mark. He was part of a Christian family. Tradition suggests it was in his house that the Upper Room of the Last Supper was located. He was probably one of those children who had been kissed by Jesus and hung around when the Master was in Jerusalem. He was also the cousin of St Barnabas. When he was still in his teens, he volunteered to accompany St Paul and his cousin on their missionary journey. Perhaps he had a vocation to be an apostle as well...

But on his arrival in Cyprus he seemingly felt that he was unable to carry on any further and went back to Jerusalem, abandoning St Paul and St Barnabas. He was not strong enough and turned back. Maybe he didn't see the mission very clearly and decided to go back home.

This fact affected St Paul and Barnabas, as well as some others who probably travelled with them. John Mark himself would, no doubt, also have felt down. He had heard from Jesus that *"no one who puts his hand to the plough and looks back is fit for the kingdom of God"* (Lk 9:62). He would have to face the disappointment of his family who had great expectations of him. What would they think? What would they say...?

St Paul was so badly affected by this episode that when the young man decided to come back and join him and Barnabas in their next missionary journey, St Paul wouldn't hear of it. Barnabas, however, took John Mark with him and so Paul and Barnabas split.

In time Mark proved he could be an apostle. Today we call him St Mark the Evangelist, the author of the second Gospel. St Mark changed his ways. He became a great collaborator of St Paul (*Philemon* 24). St Paul wrote to the Colossians that Mark gave him deep consolation (*Col* 4:10-11) and also asked Timothy to go with Mark to see him: "*Luke alone is with me. Get Mark and bring him with you; for he is very useful in serving me*" (2 Tim 4:11). St Peter was also assisted by St Mark. By the end of his life he was so fond of Mark that he even calls him "*my son*" (1 Peter 5:13).

It was the same man. He had a vocation to be an apostle. But in his first trial it seems like he didn't put everything into it. St Mark had given up easily; St Barnabas, however, hadn't. St Barnabas was a man who could spot talent. He had made of St Paul a great Apostle and he was also right about St Mark. He was there to encourage his younger cousin to try again. St Mark tried seriously a second time and proved he could become a saint by following his vocation.

There are many ways to try. Imagine someone has a talent for athletics. He is a good runner; people think he could make it as a professional. To find out, he needs to do some trials where he performs in front of a professional coach and the expert can tell whether he has what it takes to become a professional athlete.

But if he goes to the trial on the first day after his holidays, when he has done no more than eating pizzas and burgers, relaxing while sipping fizzy drinks in a hammock, one thing is for sure: he is not going to perform at his best. He will probably be rejected. Yet, he would never know whether it was because he couldn't make it as a professional or because he wasn't fit for the trials.

To get ready for those trials, he would need to train and get fit. If he is in perfect shape after weeks of training and still can't make it, then it is clear: professional athletics is not for him.

In the same way, when we try a particular vocation, we need to be committed. How do we know if this is our vocation or not? Easy – we have to try to live up to it; but try hard. If that vocation is, for instance, to a celibate life, with a particular plan of life, then we try to live it with real effort: we pray as we should; attend Holy Mass the best we can; pray the Holy Rosary as we would be expected to...

If after doing all we are supposed to do, to the best of our ability, our spiritual guide doesn't see us fit for the challenge, then we may have a different calling. Clearly, it is not a problem of generosity. However, if we are not up to par simply because we didn't pray as we should or attend Holy Mass or work as we were supposed to, then we will never know whether we failed because we didn't try or because we have a different vocation.

Whatever vocation we think could be ours, if our spiritual guide thinks we could give it a try, let's make sure that we do it with genuine effort to test it, not just have a stab at it and try our luck.

Don't be like the wuss of a bullfighter who, when he saw a huge bull running into the ring, wouldn't get 20 yards within range of the beast. After a while, the spectators started booing and shouting. One voice rose above the others and yelled, "*Come on, man! Get close to the bull!*" To which the bullfighter replied with a shaky voice, "*I'm not the problem... It's the bull who doesn't want to come near me!*"

Mary, my Mother, help me to find out what my vocation is, and to try to live it with courage, with determination, with sincere endeavour, with personal commitment.

30

What if I say "No"?

> *Mary said to the angel, "How can this be, since I have no husband?" And the angel said to her, "The Holy Spirit will come upon you, and the power of the Most High will overshadow you; therefore the child to be born will be called holy, the Son of God. And behold, your kinswoman Elizabeth in her old age has also conceived a son; and this is the sixth month with her who was called barren. For with God nothing will be impossible." And Mary said, "Behold, I am the handmaid of the Lord; let it be to me according to your word"* (Lk 1:34-38).

We have agreed on the idea that we are free. God doesn't impose His vocation on you. He asks. We can say 'Yes' or we can say 'No'. But have you ever considered the consequences of it? What if Mary had said 'No'?

The question may seem a bit bold. How could anyone suggest that the Blessed Virgin Mary, the holiest human person (remember that Jesus is a Divine Person) could have left us high and dry like that? Alright, but... what if she had? Could Mary have said 'No'? Some people might say that she was *far too holy* to say 'No'. But then, if Our Lady couldn't say 'No', she wouldn't be free. If Mary couldn't say 'No', she was forced to say 'Yes'. In that case, the most important decision in the history of the world wouldn't have been a decision as such, but a fact (like the law of gravity) which can't be any other way. At the same time, it wouldn't have had any merit if it was absolutely effortless, if she couldn't help saying 'Yes'.

Freedom is there all the time. Otherwise, if God really wants us to do something He can always sweep us off our feet the way He (supposedly) would have done with Our Lady. What makes Mary the greatest saint after God Himself is the fact that she could have said 'No' to God but she said 'Yes' instead.

Now imagine the life of Mary of Nazareth if she hadn't become the Mother of Our Lord. Here we have the most talented human person in history, an Immaculate Lady with all the perfections that God would like to give to His Mother. Because you need to understand this: Mary had all the perfections that the Mother of God needed. Those talents and gifts were not granted to Mary *after* she accepted her mission in life. She was born with them because she was born for *it*.

Picture Mary, aged 15 or 16, fetching water from the well in Nazareth. Imagine what people thought about her and how some ladies felt a bit jealous of Anna and Joaquim, because of the daughter they had. How people talked about her! What would they say? Imagine how people felt in her gracious presence, how other young girls looked for her, loved to talk with her and become friends with her. Think of St Joseph, maybe about 18 or 19 years old. How would he look at Mary and feel in her presence?

You get the point. We are talking about the most charitable, sublime, gracious, gentle, delicate, humble, strong, healthy, faithful, steadfast, honest, sensitive, sensible (perfect!) human person in history. And she was *all that* before the Archangel St Gabriel met her.

And now think, *what if she had said 'No'?* What if she had preferred to remain a simple and average lady of Nazareth? Would that not be an easier life for her? She had read the Scriptures and knew what God planned for the Messiah, the sufferings that the Messiah would bring to those who loved Him, His persecution, betrayal, Passion and death. It is certainly not what a young girl would plan for her future.

Think, for instance, of Michelangelo Buonarroti, the famous artist. Imagine that he found it difficult to hit the chisel with the hammer for hours against a block of marble and decided instead that he wanted to be a banker and make money in an easier way. Imagine that Messi found it very tiring to wake up early in the morning to go training every day and decided instead to open a garage and repair cars. Imagine that Rafa Nadal didn't like to tour around the world playing tennis in championships and even less, to follow a diet and not be able to eat what he fancied and drink fizzy drinks like everyone else, so he decided to buy a farm and grow cereal.

The picture is the same. These three examples and many more that could come to our mind speak for themselves. They were made for greatness, for excellence. Instead they could have settled for mediocrity, showing no interest in complicating their lives. They could have preferred the easy way.

But... could they be satisfied with their lives, knowing they could have been recognised as renowned artists or sportsmen but decided to choose an easier path? Let's remember what we considered earlier: *'easy'* and *'happy'* are incompatible concepts. If life is *easy*, it is not *happy*. If life is *happy*, it is not *easy*. However, these three persons in the examples didn't become famous because they *had to*, since they had those talents. They did it because they loved it!

When considering Our Lady, some people might have the opinion that she didn't have to think much to accept the Archangel's offer, that she was inclined to obey God. But that idea doesn't wash. What God wanted was not Mary's thoughtless compliance but her full, informed and free assent. When she said *"Behold the handmaid of the Lord,"* she didn't mean, *'whatever!'* This reply of Our Lady is a full acceptance, a total assent, a perfect 'Yes' which involves her entire life.

There is an essential truth that Our Lady's vocation (and ours) teaches us about God Himself. The Almighty Father creates Heaven and earth, the sun and all the stars; but when He really wants something done, He comes, the Omnipotent and Omniscient, to one of His poor, weak creatures and He asks for help.

And, day by day, He keeps on asking His creatures for help.

Will I also say: 'Your Will be done'?

Holy Mary, Handmaid of the Lord, teach me to say always with you, *"be it done unto me according to thy Word."*

31

This is not just about you

> *And Mary said, "My soul magnifies the Lord, and my spirit rejoices in God my Saviour, for he has regarded the low estate of his handmaiden. For behold, henceforth all generations will call me blessed; for he who is mighty has done great things for me, and holy is his name"* (Lk 1:46-49).

In the previous chapter we reflected on the fact that Mary *could* have said 'No' to St Gabriel's proposition. We considered the consequences that her refusal would have had in her life, her future and her happiness, the waste of her talents and gifts. We can now meditate on a second effect of that possible rejection: the consequences that her refusal would have on us.

What would St Gabriel have done if Our Mother had said 'No'? He couldn't have just gone and asked someone else, like trying to find a *second-best* option. With all the genealogies and prophecies in the Bible, there was only one candidate.

Encrypted, like a WhatsApp message, the Archangel could only deliver the communication to Mary. If she had said 'No', God would have had to change plans. That takes time and it also involves asking other people – who are also free to say 'Yes' or 'No'. If the first attempt at redemption took a few thousand years to prepare, from the Sin of Adam and Eve to the Annunciation, how many tens of thousands of years would the next attempt have taken?

Very likely, one of the thoughts that came to Our Lady's mind during the Annunciation was the multitude of people who depended on her reply. *'If I say "No",'* she might have thought, *'what's going to happen to all those who need forgiveness for their sins, the hope of salvation, the virtue of charity... all those souls who are meant to become children of God?'* This same consideration has to spur us on as well. In the words of St Josemaría, "*Many great things depend – don't forget it – on whether you and I live our lives as God wants.*"

The question, therefore, is not just, "*What could happen* to me *if I say 'No'?*" the real question is, "*What would happen* 'to us', 'to them', 'to everyone else' *if I said 'No'?*" How true are these other words of St Josemaría: "*these world crises are crises of saints.*" The world is craving holiness. We just can't afford to lose one more saint right now. For a long time, the Church, as a team, has already been short of too many players.

God has given you a vocation to make you a saint. But remember: this vocation has been given to you because *'we'* need you. Your vocation is therefore also 'ours' in a way. Meditate on those who are expecting your generous response, who hope that you will help them to fulfil their vocations as well.

As a young man, St John Vianney undertook studies for the priesthood but he found them extremely difficult. Faced with these and many other difficulties, he decided to give up on his studies for priesthood and to do something else with his life. He loved God very dearly; he just thought he wasn't made for the priesthood.

Fr Charles Balley [1751-1817] was his parish priest and knew him well; his talents, his abilities and, most of all, his love for God and zeal for souls. When the young lad made Fr Balley know his intention to leave his studies, the parish priest wouldn't hear of it. Instead, he made use of a very effective device which would guide John into reconsidering his decision. He said to him, "*This is not only about you. If you give up now, you are saying* 'goodbye priesthood' *but you are also saying* 'goodbye souls'."

Those words pierced the young lad's heart like lightning, echoing in his ears: "*goodbye souls!*" Fr Balley, like a good musician, knew which strings he had to pluck to make that instrument of God play music that has not stopped since. From that moment on, St John Mary Vianney devoted every ounce of his effort to achieving that goal and becoming the priest that thousands of souls needed.

Within ten years of his assignment to Ars (a small rural village with 230 inhabitants) he heard an average of three hundred confessions daily. In the year 1858 an estimated 100,000 pilgrims flocked to Ars. The Curé began hearing confessions at 1 o'clock in the morning, and he spent from 13 to 17 hours a day in the cramped confessional.

One day, when he was performing the exorcism of a possessed woman, the devil howled, "*If there were three people like you on earth, my kingdom would be destroyed. You have snatched more than 80,000 souls from me.*" That's a large round number, isn't it?

Do you remember the film '*It's a Wonderful Life*'? The film stars James Stewart as George Bailey, a man who is thinking about killing himself when his guardian angel Clarence (Henry Travers) appears to him. Clarence shows George all the lives he has touched and how different the world would be if he had never been there.

Our lives touch many other lives. And that is part of God's plans. Can you imagine the number of lives you can touch with God's help, bringing happiness to those lives here on earth and then, for all eternity?

Could you ever imagine a better compliment than to hear the enemy saying that you have snatched from his hands hundreds, thousands of souls?

"There are many people around you, and you have no right to be an obstacle to their spiritual good, to their eternal happiness. You are under an obligation to be a saint. You must not let God down for having chosen you. Neither must you let those around you down: they expect so much from your Christian life" (St Josemaría).

Mary, Mother of the Church, our generation is craving for saints, the Holy Church is feeling the pinch; with your intercession, Virgin Most Merciful, may many of your children never say 'No' to your Son; may we never let Him down again.

32

To fly high

> "A man ran up and knelt before him and asked him, "Good Teacher, what must I do to inherit eternal life?" And Jesus said to him, "...You know the commandments..." And he said to him, "Teacher, all these I have kept from my youth." And Jesus, looking at him, loved him, and said to him, "You lack one thing: go, sell all that you have and give to the poor, and you will have treasure in heaven; and come, follow me." Disheartened by the saying, he went away sorrowful, for he had great possessions" (Mk 10:17-22).

Before Jesus could lay this young man's vocation in front of him, He had to make sure that some prerequisites were met. That is why Jesus began checking that the young man fulfilled some preliminary conditions. If the lad didn't fulfil the commandments, it was going to be impossible for him to follow Jesus as an Apostle.

The boy confirmed that he had actually fulfilled those commandments since he was young. But when Jesus, after giving him a look full of love, called the man to follow Him, it was clear that some other requirements were not met; in this case, his attachment to riches.

We have meditated on this before: in order to listen to God's calling and respond with the affirmative, we need to climb up towards holiness. Christian struggle for holiness has been described many times as the ascent to the peak of a high mountain. Our approach to God is always upwards. If we want to give a serious thought to our vocation, we need to raise our game, as they say.

At the end of the day, it does not refer only to the amount of things that we can *do* for God. It involves, essentially, our proximity to God Himself, our intimacy with Him, our life of prayer. In short, to see your vocation, you must fly high.

As a way to describe it, we could say that our vocation is in the valley. We can only see it from the top of the mountain.

When someone says that they can't see what God wants from them, it may be the consequence of being in a position from which we cannot see. It is not God who doesn't want to reveal it yet; it is us who can't see from where we are.

The same applies when, with the passage of time, some people find themselves confused and unable to see their vocation anymore. It could be that God wants to test our fidelity; but most of the time, it is a consequence of lukewarmness in our response to it. We have gone down, so to speak, and increased our distance from God, Who is at the top, and from our current position we can't see our vocation anymore.

In those cases, it is enough to climb back up, to get out of that state of lukewarmness, to get close to God, stepping up a gear in our life of prayer, our Eucharistic devotion; and once we are higher, we can see again what we saw before.

When, after a period of consideration, people discover their vocation, they might realise that they have been on a trip towards the summit of the mountain. They have consistently looked after their daily prayer, their Holy Mass, their rosary, their devotions, precisely because they were asking God for light.

So when time wears on and, for some, their vocation wears off, it is not difficult to admit that they have put a bit of distance between themselves and God. In those times, it is easy to remember the state of our souls when we saw our vocation. If we want to see our vocation again, we need to climb back up.

A girl had spent a good number of months thinking about her vocation. She had many long talks with her spiritual director about it and still nothing was clear to her. After a while, her spiritual director gave up. She decided not bring up the topic of vocation anymore and centred their conversations on other matters. The lady thought she had said all that she could say and all that was missing was what God alone could say to the girl in her prayer.

Unexpectedly, one morning the girl went looking for her director to tell her that she had made up her mind to follow God as a celibate Christian in the middle of the world.

"*But... what changed,*" asked the spiritual director, "*to make up your mind?*"

"*Last night,*" the girl replied, "*I prayed like never before!*"

We don't know why the girl hadn't ever prayed before as she should have. But we can tell she had moved forward in that relationship with God.

St John of the Cross wrote a literary masterpiece on this topic. It is called "*The Ascent Of Mount Carmel.*" There you can read the following verses: "*I went out seeking love, and with unfaltering hope, I flew so high, so high, that I overtook the prey.*" He describes the ascent in different stages. We don't need to describe it here, but thinking about the rich young man, we could meditate on our own personal ascent.

Here is where the rubber meets the road. Let's examine our life. It is very important to be honest answering the following question: *Am I moving forward or am I stuck?* Because if there is no progress, we are not close to Him.

If that were the case, if we were not moving forward, then let's keep asking ourselves: How can I raise my game? Am I getting closer to Jesus Christ with my current life of prayer? Like the rich young man, ask Jesus what is missing. What is the next move He is expecting from me?

There may be many things that we need to change: lack of consistency in our prayer, lack of love for Jesus in the Eucharist, lack of piety, lack of good use of time, lack of mortification, lack of generosity with other people, lack of charity... or too much pride, too much vanity, too much laziness, too many susceptibilities, too many resentments and grudges... Let's not lose heart. It's O.K. We are human; let's move on! Let's just choose one thing we can change today, our next move, and move on.

Make sure you go to Our Lady now. She is the help that you need to step up that gear, to push you forward and get you higher and closer to her Son, Jesus Christ, who is calling you from the summit.

33

Destroy the ships

> *Jesus said to him, "No one who puts his hand to the plough and looks back is fit for the kingdom of God"* (Lk 9:62).

In other words, once you see what God is asking of you, go for it *full tilt*. The example we have received from the saints has always been the same. They had miseries and defects; they made mistakes and had to begin again; they faced difficulties of all kinds. But only those who persevered became what God was asking them to become.

In the First Book of Kings you find the amusing story of the calling of the prophet Elisha. He was working in the fields when the Prophet Elijah found him with his hands on the plough. "*There were twelve yoke of oxen ahead of him, and he was with the twelfth. Elijah passed by him and threw his mantle over him.*" That was the sign that prophets used at the time to call new disciples to follow them. That was it. No more dialogue, discussion or Q&As.

Immediately, we read, Elisha *left the oxen, ran after Elijah, and said, "Let me kiss my father and my mother, and then I will follow you.*" Elijah gave him permission to say goodbye to his family and Elisha went back. However, Elisha didn't just say goodbye to his family. We read something remarkable in the Scripture text: he "*took the yoke of oxen, and slaughtered them; using the equipment from the oxen, he boiled their flesh, and gave it to the people, and they ate. Then he set out and followed Elijah, and became his servant*" (1 *Kg* 19:19-21).

That was it! He took the oxen and prepared a barbecue using the yoke for the fire! That's a radical way to 'burn the ships', to mark a point of no return. In this way, Elisha made sure that he wouldn't have the temptation to come back because there was nothing left. No longer was there anything behind him; everything was now in front of him.

In 1519 Hernan Cortes set sail to Veracruz (Mexico) with his crew. Upon arrival, Cortes' men became weary and scared, with hopes of turning back home to their old life. Cortes then had the men destroy and sink their ships (legend says he burned them up with rum). That way, they were left with no option but to press on. No going back; their safety net had been removed.

The burning of those ships represented much more than a separation from their old ways. If they had in the back of their minds the possibility of going back, they would be hesitating the whole time and never committed one hundred per cent. The same fire that set the ships ablaze also allowed Cortes' men to complete their mission and be a part of something greater than themselves.

There is an important point to be remembered by someone who decides to say 'Yes' to God and follow his or her vocation: '*Satan hates your vocation.*' That's no news. He hates you and me, your vocation and mine, so he will never give up in his mission to discourage anyone from serving God. All the saints have had to fight to persevere to the end. That's why they are saints. As

St Josemaría puts it: "*To begin is for everyone. To persevere is for saints.*"

To make resolutions is for everyone. To keep them is for saints. In fact, every resolution, if it is to happen, is a double resolution. It involves doing something and not giving up until it's done. Perseverance is a virtue that attracts everyone. It is a virtue in every culture.

Do you remember 'The Two Towers', the second part of the production 'The Lord of the Rings'? There is a moment when Frodo is about to give up. He says to his faithful friend, Sam Gamgee, "*I can't do this, Sam.*" To encourage his companion, Sam invites him to remember the acts of the heroes in good stories.

"*It's like in the great stories, Mr. Frodo,*" Sam says, "*the ones that really mattered. Full of darkness and danger, they were. And sometimes you didn't want to know the end. Because how could the end be happy? How could the world go back to the way it was when so much bad had happened? But in the end, it's only a passing thing, this shadow. Even darkness must pass. A new day will come. And when the sun shines it will shine out the clearer. Those were the stories that stayed with you. That meant something, even if you were too small to understand why.*"

Then Sam explains the important point of those stories: "*But I think, Mr. Frodo, I do understand. I know now. Folk in those stories had lots of chances of turning back, only they didn't. They kept going. Because they were holding on to something.*" "*What are we holding on to, Sam?*" asks Frodo. "*That there's some good in this world, Mr. Frodo,*" Sam replies, "*and it's worth fighting for.*"

That is the point: "*Folk in those stories had lots of chances of turning back, only they didn't. They kept going.*" Saints had every chance of giving up, only they didn't. Because they were holding on to God's promises and His grace.

Saints had many chances to take their hands off the plough, many reasons to complain, to say 'Enough', to say 'No'. But they didn't. And that is why we call them saints.

Mary, Virgin Most Faithful, I count on your assistance. Help me to never give up and to persevere with determination so that I can fulfil God's Will until the very last moment of my life.

34

You raise me up

> *The God who girded me with strength and kept my way safe, He made my feet like hinds' feet, and set me secure on the heights* (Psalm 18).

- O.K. Agreed. *In order to see and follow our vocation, we need to raise our game. We know we need to improve some aspects of our lives and set up a plan of struggle. But the fact that we know what must be done and how to do it, doesn't make things any easier.*

Certainly. But here is all you need to know: *God is the One Who raises your game.*

- *Is that all?*

That's it. It sounds simple and it IS simple. This is what we learn from the lives of the saints. They climbed up to the heights of holiness in God's Hands. Many saints explained it in different ways, but the gist of all their descriptions is the same: 1) They knew they **couldn't do** it by themselves; and 2) they were convinced God **could do** it.

Do you remember the song '*You Raise Me Up*'? It became a great hit in 2003. Here you have the lyrics: *When I am down, and, oh, my soul, so weary / When troubles come, and my heart burdened be / Then, I am still and wait here in the silence / Until you come and sit awhile with me / You raise me up, so I can stand on mountains / You raise me up to walk on stormy seas / I am strong when I am on your shoulders; You raise me up to more than I can be* (Brendan Graham).

It's not Holy Scripture but the lyrics match the doctrines of many mystics like those of St Teresa or St John of the Cross. We are weak, *'weary'*; we all feel troubles and some of them can burden our hearts. It is no time to get worried. It is time to pray: *"Then, I am still and wait here in the silence."* That is prayer: when God longs to *"sit awhile with me."*

And there the miracle happens. There, in the Presence of God, looking at the Eucharistic Face of God, conversing with Him, spending time with Him... there we are raised up, up high, over those issues that trouble us, over our miseries, over our limitations, over our bad experiences of life, over our comfort-seeking addiction, over our tendency to fall, our sensuality, our laziness, our discouragements, our defeats, our vices, our pride, our vanity: God raises us up higher than all of our sins.

Stop for a moment and meditate on this: *'God can raise your game higher than you could ever imagine.'*

The saints understood it; they believed it; they saw it. They were *strong*, as the song goes, because they were, like little children, on their Father's Shoulders. Then, they could stand on mountains, on stormy seas and on any trouble that could bother them. Do you understand the trick? Saints were not taller; they were on God's Shoulders.

Think about the launch of a rocket. It takes a lot of energy to take it outside the atmosphere, to accelerate to orbital speed, to overcome the attraction of gravity, and the resistance of the air.... That's why they always carry huge tanks of fuel. We could think that, to raise us up, God could act like a rocket or a powerful catapult. However, rockets can't choose, they aren't free, they can't cooperate. They are lifeless, inert objects.

To explain this ascension to the heights of perfection and love for God, St Josemaría preferred to describe the flight of a bird. Have you ever seen the majestic flight of a bird of prey – an eagle for instance? They can soar up without beating their wings, without toil, until they disappear behind the clouds. It would be impossible for a sparrow or a hummingbird to reach the heights of an eagle just by beating their wings.

Many people think that it is all about their wingspan. But it is not just that. Two other important conditions allow eagles to soar in the skies: 1) their bodies are very light compared to their size; and 2) they use the wind currents.

We meditated on the first condition earlier when we read the story of the rich young man. He had good intentions but he also had many possessions - so much dead weight. The Apostles could follow Jesus because they travelled with the few items they had. That was our first lesson: in order to fly high, you need to get rid of dead weight, everything that God doesn't need, all that material junk that keeps us anchored to earth. This Christian virtue is called *detachment*.

However, getting rid of material things is not enough. We also need those currents of favourable winds. And we get those in the Presence of the Eucharistic Face of God. We find in the Eucharist the energy we need to fly; and also from the Eucharist, we get those winds that can lift us up.

"I see myself like a poor little bird," St Josemaría wrote, *"accustomed only to making short flights from tree to tree, or, at most, up to a third floor balcony. One day in its life it succeeded in reaching the roof of a modest building, that you could hardly call a skyscraper. And lo and behold, our little bird is snatched up by an eagle, who mistakes the bird for one of its own brood. In its powerful talons the*

bird is borne higher and higher, above the mountains of the earth and the snow-capped peaks, above the white, blue and rose-pink clouds, and higher and higher until it can look right into the sun. And then the eagle lets go of the little bird and says, 'Off you go. Fly!' Lord, may I never flutter again close to the ground. May I always be enlightened by the rays of the divine sun - Christ - in the Eucharist. May my flight never be interrupted until I find repose in your Heart."

It is not, then, about getting exhausted beating our tiny wings. Relying only on our human resources won't get us very far. By ourselves we can't raise our game, overcome our defects, get the virtues that we need... All that the little sparrow will manage to do by beating its wings is to tire out. Only God can make us soar. We need to spend time in God's Presence, in adoration, without giving up.

But remember: God can't do it without our cooperation. We are like the bird, not like the rocket. It is not just the wings, not just the winds, but the eagle *with* the winds. Likewise, it won't be you alone, it won't be God alone... To raise us up, we have to combine our human efforts with God's grace.

Let us ask Our Lady, Full of Grace, for her intercession to bring us close to her Son, Jesus Christ present in the Eucharist. There, spending time with Him, we will feel those currents of hot air; and if we persevere, He will raise us up.

35

To fill the gap

> *Moses said to them: "I am now one hundred and twenty years old. I am no longer able to get about, and the Lord has told me, 'You shall not cross over this Jordan.' The Lord your God himself will cross over before you... Then Moses summoned Joshua and said to him in the sight of all Israel: "Be strong and bold, for you are the one who will go with this people into the land that the Lord has sworn to their ancestors to give them; and you will put them in possession of it. It is the Lord who goes before you. He will be with you; he will not fail you or forsake you. Do not fear or be dismayed"* (Deut 31:2-3;7-8).

On 1942 Jose Luis was twelve years old. His family was spending Christmas at the house of his uncle, Don Cosme, his mother's brother and priest of San Cebrian de Arriba, a village in León (Spain). A heavy snowfall was falling on the night of 27 to 28 December when the noise of a horse approaching interrupted the peaceful silence.

A man knocked at the door and informed the priest that, in the neighbouring village, a lady was very ill and about to die that night. After informing the priest, the man turned around and went on his way elsewhere, looking for a doctor. Don Cosme did not hesitate. His sister tried to dissuade him from going out at night in the snow and walking the three miles that separated the two little towns. She only managed to persuade him to take his twelve-year-old nephew, Jose Luis, with him. He wrote his recollections a few years later:

"The snow had stopped and the air was lukewarm. The moon gave the snow a strangely white light. When we left the village, the clocktower struck 10pm. My uncle was wrapped in his cloak, under which he hid his box containing the Sacraments. The first part of the road was easy; but after a while the moon hid and it began to snow again. The cold was now piercing and made my eyes water. The night became very dark and I became very afraid; I felt my feet sinking more than ever. We lost all signs of the path. I looked at my uncle without daring to speak and saw in his eyes the same fear that I was feeling. We stopped. The snow had covered everything and there was no way to guess where the ground was firm."

"We continued to walk randomly; now the fear was in my heart. And that's when it happened. My uncle lost his footing and fell with a scream. I tried to help him stand up - but it was useless. He could not stand and would never walk again. The rest all happened very quickly. I ran like a madman to the village, not minding about the danger that I could also run into. I pounded on the door of the first house until my knuckles hurt. The news spread from house to house, and in a moment about twenty men and several dogs accompanied me to the place where I had left my uncle. It was still snowing and only the dogs' barking broke the silence. My uncle was unconscious, but still alive. When they lifted him up I could see blood staining the whiteness of the snow. Wrapped in a blanket, they brought him to the village. He opened his eyes and asked to be taken to the sick lady's home."

"They brought him next to the fire and he revived little by little while the doctor bandaged his leg. When he recovered slightly, he asked to be brought next to the bed of the lady in need, a wrinkled old woman who spoke in quick outbursts. There was a crowd in the room, and I noticed that they all had their lips tightened as if to keep from crying. I stood by the stove, not quite understanding what was going on. It was all too big for my little head. My uncle and the old lady seemed to never get tired of talking. I could hear my uncle's muffled breath – an irregular breath, like the sound of a broken machine. Then, somehow, I saw him like one of those logs in the fire that slowly bends until at last it falls… But even now his clear smile did not fade. It was his joy to be dying in an act of service, dying exhausted but warming others up, giving his place to another log that would come after him, replacing him until it would be his turn to die also in the fire. That's when the sudden thought struck me: 'Why could I not be the wood that should replace him?'"

"The next day the bells of the two villages tolled death, although it seemed to me that they were tolling glory. I was self-absorbed, withdrawn. People thought I was sad about the death of my uncle, but how could I be saddened by such a great death? That death seemed so terribly beautiful to me that I started to wish it for myself. And it was this wish that haunted my childish brain."

The following October, Jose Luis entered the seminary. Things were not easy, but he was determined. "*I always remembered my uncle in every priest that I saw and recalled that snowy night whenever our courtyard appeared in white; I remembered especially that stove where logs were consumed and I thought: one day I will be the one burning in the fire, giving warmth and light. What would become of us without this life-giving fire? Villages without a priest – I thought – must be like a perpetual winter."*

"When I finished my first Mass, I sat in a corner of the church and stayed there for a long time, as if trying to explain to myself what had *happened. Everything in my life was different. I was starting to feel useful and my life began to count for something. I looked at myself among men with my hands full of love, being a channel between them and God; a channel that would rain down graces from Heaven and raise up their prayers from the earth. I could see myself pouring holy water on the foreheads of children, accompanying the dying in their last minutes, forgiving the sins of the youth and, ah, watching them leave happy, with a new joy – and blessing new homes in which life would perpetuate. I saw children kneeling, pure and angelic, before the altar, and myself bringing Our Lord's Body down to them and putting Him on their tongues; praying for the dead, my blessing being the last thing descending on their graves between shovels of earth; blessing houses, animals and fruits, and speaking to people about God; and for all of them, I raised in my hands the White Host, in which Christ would show Himself to us and come to live among us. Yes, I thought; my life is beginning to count for something."*

"I think I'm burning now; I'm the log in the fire, the fire that gives light and warms others up. That is my destiny: to be consumed in a glorious act of service to men. And I'm so proud of this destiny! For how long? It doesn't matter. Maybe many years, like my uncle; perhaps a few months, maybe a few days; who knows if tonight it will start to snow and the road will be covered in white – and a rider on horseback will come and knock on my door? So I have to hurry; I have to find someone to replace me, who will keep the fire burning if I die. This fire cannot be extinguished because, without it, the world would not stand."

Mary, Mother of the Church, may we never lack generosity to be ready to give ourselves up, like a log in the fire, to give light and warmth to others and to bring more logs to the bonfire.

36

How can I be 100% sure?

> *Now the eleven disciples went to Galilee, to the mountain to which Jesus had directed them. And when they saw him they worshiped him; but some doubted* (Mt 28:16, 17).

It is striking that, after the Resurrection of Our Lord, there was still a number of them who were in doubt. But about what? Was it not enough for them to see the scars of the Passion on Jesus' Hands and Feet? What else did they need to see? His passport and birth certificate? And if Jesus was to produce His passport... how could you tell it was not a forgery? When it comes to doubting, there are no limits. You can spend the rest of your life doubting everything and so, doing nothing.

Some people spend years praying about vocation and never get anywhere. As St Josemaría put it, they may be expecting an Angel to come from Heaven and use one of his feathers to sign a document issuing their vocation officially and without room for error. They want to be sure. They want to play safe.

If you read the lives of the saints and their accounts about their own vocations you never find a visible sign, an apparition, a few words coming from Heaven. Even those saints who *did* hear the Voice of God, those who *saw* Jesus or Mary in apparitions, those who got special revelations... all of them had those extraordinary interventions from Heaven AFTER they had followed their vocations.

There are two very interesting exceptions to this 'rule'. St Bernadette and Sister Lucia dos Santos. They both had apparitions of Our Lady before they followed their religious vocations. They were still girls when Our Lady revealed to them many things: about herself, about the future, about the Will of God... Is it not remarkable that Our Lady didn't reveal their vocations to them? Think about it:

Our Lady comes down from Heaven to ask for prayers and reparation for sinners, to ask us to say her Rosary. In the course of those conversations she is very affectionate with the children and promises them that, if they cooperate with their special graces, they will go to Heaven. As we now know, God wanted St Bernadette and Sister Lucia to become religious nuns. Our Lady knew it when she talked to them. Would it not be a sign of maternal care to let them know their vocations and spare them the long process of discernment?

When Lucia asked Our Lady of Fatima if she would take them to Heaven, Our Lady replied, *"I will take Jacinta and Francisco soon. But you are to stay here some time longer. Jesus wishes to make use of you to make me known and loved. He wants to establish in the world devotion to my Immaculate Heart."* Hearing that, Lucia was sad and asked, "*Am I to stay here alone?"* Our Mother consoled her, *"No, my daughter. Are you suffering a great deal? Don't lose heart. I will never forsake you. My Immaculate Heart will be your refuge and the way that will lead you to God."* Our Lady said many things about the future but she never mentioned that God wanted Lucia to become a nun.

Why? To respect her freedom. God loves our freedom. He freed us by paying a very expensive ransom with all His Blood. He wants us to follow Him because we love Him, not because we have to. To follow our vocation we need faith, trust in God. And faith is only possible when we don't have a self-evident certainty. You don't have faith in the fact that you are alive. You know it.

If God were to certify your vocation sending an Angel with an official document of divine vocation, what room would there be to have faith in God? But even more importantly: how could you say 'No'? It would be very 'difficult' to say to the Angel ambassador, *'Listen, thanks but... I'll pass on this one'*. If it is impossible to say 'No', then there is no perfect freedom.

One of the most famous lines from the film *'The Godfather'* (1972) comes from the mouth of don Vito Corleone (Marlon Brando). When his godson Johnny Fontane comes crying to him because he hasn't been offered a role in a film, Corleone tells him, *"I'll make him an offer he can't refuse."* This line became very popular because of the effect it has: an offer, by definition, can be refused. If it can't be refused then it is not an offer, it's a command.

Our vocation is an invitation from God, an offer. And as it happens with all proper invitations, we are free to accept it or not. God makes sure that, when He makes the offer, we can refuse at any point – because we are free. For this reason God doesn't send His Angels (or even His Mother) to reveal our vocation to us.

Therefore, there is always room for doubt. Those who want to spend the rest of their lives doubting can choose to do that with perfect freedom. One can never be certain of a divine calling on one particular day, all of a sudden. It is a discovery that grows within your soul when you spend time in dialogue with God. Don't expect a supernatural dazzling light, an emotional angelic soundtrack and a feeling of the overwhelming power of divine love wrapping your soul and eliciting tears... because it may not happen.

In fact, when you read what the saints had to say about their vocations, you find very little romanticism. They usually don't offer proper descriptions of the moment of their discovery. Somehow, it just happens. One day they 'knew', and that was it.

St John Paul II explained to a group of young people in Los Angeles on September 14, 1987: "*I am often asked, especially by young people, why I became a priest. Maybe some of you would like to ask the same question. Let me try briefly to reply. I must begin by saying that it is impossible to explain entirely. For it remains a mystery, even to myself. How does one explain the ways of God? Yet, I know that, at a certain point in my life, I became convinced that Christ was saying to me what he had said to thousands before me: 'Come, follow me!' There was a clear sense that what I heard in my heart was no human voice, nor was it just an idea of my own. Christ was calling me to serve him as a priest.*"

It was just like that: at "*a certain point*" in his life, he "*became convinced*". St Teresa of Calcutta explains that discovery of one's vocation is the fruit of silent prayer. It remains a mystery, but it is real: "*In the silence of the heart God speaks. The person whom Christ has chosen for himself, she knows. Maybe she doesn't know how to express it, but she knows.*"

Let's ask Our Lady for the faith that we need to be able to follow God's vocation and trust in Him, because even if there is no absolute certainty, God doesn't abandon His children who abandon themselves in Him.

37

The switch behind the door

> *Some people brought to him a blind man, and begged him to touch him. And he took the blind man by the hand, and led him out of the village; and when he had spit on his eyes and laid his hands upon him, he asked him, "Do you see anything?" And he looked up and said, "I see men; but they look like trees, walking." Then again he laid his hands upon his eyes; and he looked intently and was restored, and saw everything clearly* (Mk 8:22-25).

Jesus healed every person in a different way. He didn't have a protocol or a particular system. Each one had a *'personalised'* miracle. The story of this blind man is quite remarkable. Jesus spat on his eyes! Can you imagine this? Someone told the blind man that Jesus had healed other blind people before. So the man asked to be brought to Jesus and when they brought him in front of Our Lord, Jesus spat on his face.

What did the blind man do? Nothing. He waited. He trusted Jesus. He didn't understand what was going on. But he trusted Jesus. Then Jesus laid His Hands upon him and asked *"Do you see anything?"* He looked up and... he could see something, but it wasn't the miracle he was expecting. Maybe the man doubted a bit now. Perhaps his case was more difficult...

What did the blind man do? He waited. He trusted. So Jesus laid His Hands on him again, this time upon his eyes, and then the man *"looked intently and was restored, and saw everything clearly."* It was about trust. The blind man may have had doubts during the process, but he 'believed' in Jesus, so he waited until Our Lord restored his sight.

Trust is necessary to move forward. If you want to see your vocation, you need to trust. You may not understand what Jesus is doing in your life. But those doubts are not an obstacle, they are an opportunity to show how much you trust Him. Once you 'know' what God expects from you, start moving on!

There will be doubts. There is no 100% certainty. But until you trust to the point of saying 'Yes', your doubts will not fade away. We could say that in the things of God, *'the switch is behind the door'*. When you come into a dark room, you need to feel your way, groping for the switch. Our first steps in any vocation need trust, insecure short steps, fumbling about in a dark place. We move on, being aware that God is there and that He will never leave us alone, especially if we are showing trust by walking towards Him in the dark.

A boy asked his dad, *"How did you know that 'mum' was the right one?"* *"Little by little,"* said the father, *"we started dating and in a few months I realised it couldn't be anyone else."* The boy insisted, *"But when did you know for sure that she was the one - with absolute certainty?"* *"That happened at a very particular moment: I put a gold ring on her finger and, in front of the priest, swore to God that she was the one."*

With vocation, one can have the certainty proper to human beings, which is not absolute and complete. Great certainty is only achieved some time after having said 'Yes' to it. That certainty comes when we have walked the *path* for a while and we verify that treading this path satisfies our soul; only then we can reach very high degrees of certainty.

This is the same for many of our decisions in life. Think about your studies. How can you be absolutely certain that you have to study Law, or Medicine, or Philosophy? You have inklings, an inclination towards a subject... It is very easy to discard some options. Those who are a disaster in maths can rule out maths, physics, chemistry and many other subjects. It is easy to spot the options that will not work for us. The difficulty is about how to be 100% certain that your university degree has to be a particular one among a few you feel inclined towards.

In order to grow in certainty, there is another important feature: *will*. Security has a lot to do with our will, with how much we are willing to throw ourselves wholeheartedly into the project. Security is not given to us, it is achieved with our will to respond. So, it is not a problem to have doubts, like those disciples who saw Jesus Resurrected in front of them. The important thing is how we react to those doubts. If we react with trust, we will be rewarded with a prize.

This is the reason why all institutions of the Church have a trial period. Like the courtship between boyfriend and girlfriend, when they get to know each other better and see where their relationship can go. An engagement can be broken off. It can happen because the couple realise that it will never work.

However, it can also happen because one of them, or both, haven't been faithful in their relationship or haven't been committed, taken it seriously. They just didn't even try. In this case, a couple that was meant to be happy together, may never achieve the goal because they didn't have that *wilfulness*. It is then common to hear, "*I knew it wasn't meant to be...*" or "*I knew he wasn't the right guy...*" but that could be an excuse to avoid acknowledging that it was their fault, it was their lack of desire and commitment.

Of course, a soul can honestly doubt if she sees no compelling sign of her vocation. But doubts can also be voluntarily sought. We have to be honest. Those people who spend years chewing on their vocation need to know if it is because they don't see, or because they don't *want* to see, or even because they actually saw it, but don't want to say 'Yes'. In this case, they may be choosing not to say 'No' to God and instead, say nothing. God is no fool: not to say 'Yes' is a 'No'.

In a nutshell: in matters of divine calling, there is no mathematical certainty. There is always a risk. There is the risk of saying 'No' to God when He was expecting a 'Yes'. There is also the risk of saying 'Yes' to God when He was expecting from you a 'Yes' in another place. But if that were the case, do you think God would be disappointed? He will smile at your generosity. He will not leave you in error. He will lead you to the proper door you have to knock at and He will be proud of you, for trusting Him so much.

Mary, Virgin Most Prudent, help me to solve my doubts, trusting in your Son and knowing that God lavishly rewards our generosity.

38

Am I risking too much?

> "The kingdom of heaven is like treasure hidden in a field, which a man found and covered up; then in his joy he goes and sells all that he has and buys that field. Again, the kingdom of heaven is like a merchant in search of fine pearls, who, on finding one pearl of great value, went and sold all that he had and bought it" (Mt 13:44-46).

In the examples that Jesus presents here we find a similar reaction. For both men found something worth more than all they possessed. Think about the man who found the pearl of great value. He had been collecting pearls for a while and probably had a good collection already. He had many valuable pearls. But suddenly he found one that outclassed all of them and was worth more than all the previous pearls put together.

The man who found the treasure and the man who found the pearl understood that it was worth putting in everything they had to get their findings. The question is: were they risking too much? No. In fact there was no risk at all. There is risk if you don't know what the outcome is going to be, like in the lottery or in roulette. But there is no risk buying a field that has treasure in it, once you verify the chest is there and is full of jewels.

The question comes to mind when we have to find the meaning of our lives. Am I risking too much giving my whole life to God? No. In fact, there is no risk at all, since you know that there is a *Treasure* promised by God – and God never fails to fulfil His promises. That was the message of Our Lord's parable: it is worth giving up everything else to get that field which contains the treasure. That field, the one God has given you, is your vocation. It has Heaven attached to it. But to get that field, you need to go all in, to bet your whole life.

There is no risk when you are certain of the outcome. It is not like betting. It is more like shopping. You know exactly what you are getting when you pay for it. Saints have learned that. There is no risk when we know Heaven is the reward: that 'prize' is worth any 'price'.

St Frances Cabrini founded the Community of the Missionaries of the Sacred Heart in 1880. At that time there were many Italians emigrating to North America. The Archbishop of New York, Msgr. Corrigan, had personally asked St Frances to send her sisters to that country. She wanted them to go to China, but Pope Leo XIII begged her to attend to that request and St Frances immediately changed her plans. The trip was very hard and very long, but she crossed the Atlantic with six of her nuns and landed in New York in March 1889.

The reception was not exactly enthusiastic. Upon her arrival, she found that the benefactors who had promised to get a house to set up an orphanage and an elementary school had had second thoughts and the project had been called off. Bishop Corrigan was so discouraged that he ended up trying to convince St Frances that it was better for her and her sisters to go back to Italy. But she replied, "*No, Your Excellency, the Pope sent us here, and here we are going to stay.*" She could have been discouraged, but she had bet her life on it and she was not going to give up. Within a few months they had found another house and in less than a year the first two American novices were already in Italy.

The Community of Missionaries of the Sacred Heart not only settled immediately in New York, but it also began to spread throughout North and South America, with numerous schools, orphanages and hospitals. After just twenty years, there were already more than a thousand religious! St Frances Cabrini would end up being the first American citizen canonized, and her life was an example of tenacity and strength, of activity in God's service and of holy concern for the desolate and helpless youth. She took a chance on God – and wasn't disappointed.

Betting on God is not taking a risk. In fact, it is the only way to play safe with your life. You were made for happiness, eternal happiness. Giving yourself to God can guarantee that happiness. In the end, answering 'Yes' to God's call will always be an act of faith in that call and in the One who calls. And if we believe in Him, we commit our lives to Him.

Commitment? Nowadays, commitment is not a popular word. It seems that it doesn't fit in with our times any more. Commercials insist time and again that, if you don't like the product, you can always change it or ask for a refund. This *'returns policy'* has extended to such a degree that people don't like to make contracts even for their phone plans! They want to feel free to change, amend, abandon the plan and switch, any time, for another they may fancy in the future. This lack of commitment is the woodworm of happiness.

Commitment to God is the only sure path to happiness. Saints knew this. For a temporary reward, you can try any trifle. But for an everlasting, total and absolute happiness, you need to put everything into that field with the treasure. You can't pay for the field in instalments, you can't take out a mortgage, you can't ask for credit. You need to put your life at stake, commit your life and give it up to God. There is no other way.

"It is so hard in our time to make final decisions!" explains Pope Francis. *"Temporary things seduce us. We are victims of a trend that pushes us to the provisional... as though we wanted to stay adolescents. There is a little charm in staying adolescents, and this for life! Let us not be afraid of life commitments, commitments that take up and concern our entire life! In this way our life will be fruitful! And this is freedom: to have the courage to make these decisions with generosity."*

"Mary as a good mother teaches us to be, like her, capable of making definitive decisions; definitive choices, at this moment in a time controlled by, so to speak, a philosophy of the provisional. It is very difficult to make a lifetime commitment. And she helps us to make those definitive decisions in the full freedom with which she said "yes" to the plan God had for her life" (cf. Lk 1:38). (Pope Francis, St Mary Major; Saturday, 4 May 2013).

39

The prize

> *Peter began to say to him, "Lo, we have left everything and followed you." Jesus said, "Truly, I say to you, there is no one who has left house or brothers or sisters or mother or father or children or lands, for my sake and for the gospel, who will not receive a hundredfold now in this time, houses and brothers and sisters and mothers and children and lands, with persecutions, and in the age to come eternal life"* (Mk 10:28-30).

This conversation follows Our Lord's encounter with the rich young man. The young lad had been asking what was lacking for him to inherit Eternal Life and was taken aback by Our Lord's reply. He wasn't ready to get rid of his possessions and decided to say 'No' to Jesus' offer of following Him.

Peter and the others had heard the conversation. They were probably also excited by the possibility of having this new 'candidate' incorporated to their group. Jesus, says St Mark's Gospel, "*looking upon him loved him.*" And so did Peter and the others. But when the young man turned his back on them, the whole group felt a bit let down. Peter could understand Jesus' disappointment and he too felt sorry.

Then Peter attempted to cheer Our Lord up: *'Forget it, Lord'*, Peter would say. *'See! We are here and we have left everything to follow You – and we will not leave You. Lord, you can count on us!'* Jesus was probably moved by Peter's words. Imagine Jesus looking around at those men who had put everything on the line to follow Him wherever He wanted to go; loyal friends who loved Him so much.

But then Peter asked for something else: *'What shall we get?'* The interesting part for our meditation is that Jesus didn't just promise them Heaven, eternal life in the age to come. The most interesting bit is the *"hundredfold now in this time."* Our Lord is promising happiness to those who follow Him. Not just eternal happiness, but temporal happiness, here on earth. That's why the saints are the only really happy people on earth. In the words of St Josemaría, *"I am every day more convinced that happiness in Heaven is for those who know how to be happy on earth."*

As St Augustine teaches, *"There is no man who does not desire [happiness], and each one desires it with such earnestness that he prefers it to all other things; whoever, in fact, desires other things, desires them for this end alone."* This urge for happiness is as natural for us to desire as it is to breathe. We were made for happiness. That is why God made the Garden of Eden as it was. It was the happy abode that Our Father prepared for us. And that is why our hearts yearn for that happiness.

God wants your heart to make you happy as much as the devil wants it to make you miserable. And so, in this search for happiness, the enemy fools us into trying to get it with trifles. But they don't work. Man is too big to be happy with what material things can give him. A soul may try more and more until she realises that real happiness can only be achieved with *love* and not with *things*. Those who love more are happier. And nobody ever loved like the saints.

People think that saints left everything hoping to get happiness at the end, like someone who works on a project that will pay back only after it is finished. They think that Heaven is like chasing the carrot, but that's not the case. Happiness is not just the *goal*. Happiness is *the way* as well. Certainly, the happiness we aspire to, the eternal one, is beyond anything we can feel on this earth. But still, there is a lot of it here for those who love.

To follow your vocation is, then, not just a matter of justice (God deserves that we give Him everything); it is not even a favour we do for God; it is not an obligation to God either. To follow your vocation is the only way you can get the happiness that was meant for you from the beginning of creation. It is good to think about giving glory to God. But don't forget His promise: the "*hundredfold now in this time.*"

It is quite simple: God wants you to be happy and has set a way for you to get that happiness. You are free to take the whole lot or to settle for less. Maybe one of the greatest personal disasters in life is to ignore the path that God has planned to give us His happiness.

So, in the end, running away from our vocation is running away from our true happiness. St Augustine was well aware of this. He chased that worldly happiness in everything that creation could give him. He lamented at the end of his life: "*I did not love you...and all those around me who were doing the same, echoed, 'Well done! Well done!'*" Years later, remembering those times, he prayed to Our Lord thus: "*I was tossed about, and wasted, and dissipated, and I boiled over in my fornications, and Thou didst hold Thy peace, O Thou my tardy joy! Thou then didst hold Thy peace, and I wandered still further and further from Thee, into more and more fruitless seed-plots of sorrows, with a proud dejectedness, and a restless weariness.*"

St Augustine explains how our soul has an infinite capacity and infinite desire: God is infinite. But all of our human pursuits are finite, they have an end point, coming to a close with our own personal bodily death. *"This is true happiness in life,"* writes the saint, *"to take joy in you, for you, because of you – this, nothing else, is happiness. Those who do not know this pursue their joy elsewhere, and though it is no true one, yet they cannot wrench their desire entirely free from some representation of that joy... I seek the happy life."* He is talking about *La dolce vita!* Not just in Heaven, but here on earth: *"You are the happiness that everyone desires, the only happiness."*

That's why he complained about his resistance to grasp that happiness: *"Late have I loved you, Beauty so ancient and so new, late have I loved you! Lo, you were within, but I outside, seeking there for you, and upon the shapely things you have made, I rushed headlong – I, misshapen. You were with me, but I was not with you... You called, shouted, broke through my deafness; you flared, blazed, banished my blindness; you lavished your fragrance, I gasped; and now I pant for you; I tasted you, and now I hunger and thirst; you touched me, and I burned for your peace."*

Your thirst for happiness is a thirst for God, and until you give yourself entirely to Him, He can't give Himself entirely to you. The Bishop of Hippo summarises his whole life with that introduction to his Confessions: *"You have made us for Yourself, and our hearts are restless, until they can find rest in You."*

Mary, my Mother, Cause of our Joy, may I find my hundredfold in your lap, under your protection, led by your hand.

40

"Faithful in a very little, faithful also in much"

> *As Jesus said this, a woman in the crowd raised her voice and said to him, "Blessed is the womb that bore you, and the breasts that you sucked!" But he said, "Blessed rather are those who hear the word of God and keep it!"* (Lk 11:27-28).

After the Annunciation, we don't find many references to Our Lady in the Gospels. We find her at the beginning of the Gospels of Matthew and Luke when they recount the infancy of Jesus. We also find Our Mother at the end of John's Gospel, during the Passion of Our Lord. But apart from the short reference to her presence at Cana during the wedding, we don't find her mentioned much more.

So what does Jesus say about His Mother? St Luke records a few important words of Jesus which He refers to His Mother. It is the text that opens this chapter. Among the crowd of Our Lord's listeners, a woman raised her voice to shout a blessing to Jesus' Mother. It may have been quite an abrupt interruption, but Jesus would surely have liked it. He probably smiled at the lady and at the remembrance of Our Lady. The Son couldn't agree more: Mary was, indeed, blessed.

However, Jesus wanted to make a point clear. By accepting God's Will, Mary brought these blessings upon herself. Jesus tells His audience, and you and me, that Mary wasn't blessed due to her 'appointment' as Mother of God, but rather to her willingness to hear God's Word and to keep It in her Immaculate Heart.

This seems to be a constant reference of Jesus regarding His Mother. We read in the Gospel of St Matthew (12:46) and St Mark (3:33) that one day Our Lady and some relatives came to see Jesus and someone let Him know about it. He was probably very happy to have His Mother there and smiled. Then He looked around and decided to use the example of His Mother to teach His listeners a lesson. Stretching out His Hand toward His disciples, Jesus said, *"Here are my mother and my brethren! For whoever does the will of my Father in heaven is my brother, and sister, and mother."* As if saying, 'The most important feature of my Mother is that she does the Will of my Father.'

We are not told much about the trials and challenges of Our Lady's life, but we are reminded by Jesus Himself that she fulfilled God's Will. She didn't say 'Yes' just once. She said 'Yes' all her life. When it was the Will of God to change her plans, she adapted herself to It. That is the mark of holiness.

Not all the things God asked His Mother to do were of the same importance. But as Jesus Himself taught, *"Whoever is faithful in a very little is faithful also in much"* (Lk 16:10). Those who do what God asks them to do are in a position to be asked more. We can't expect to give ourselves to God in a celibate life if we are unable to 'give ourselves to God' by getting up in the morning, or by saying our prayers in the evening. If we can't fulfil God's Will in little things, how are we going to give Him the big ones?

At the start of the foundation of Opus Dei, St Josemaría needed the support of other people. In a few years, a group of young students and professionals gathered around him and he began sharing the burden of the government of the incipient institution.

As he was entrusting diverse tasks and jobs to different people, some were more diligent than others. It was not a matter of commitment. They were all committed. But some had more ability than others to resolve matters, tackle issues and follow things up. Some people had more spare time to devote to those tasks whilst others were more heavily involved in their professional work and duties.

In time, St Josemaría wanted to rely on a particular person to be with him all the time, governing the Work with him. He found himself delegating more and more to a young civil engineer called Alvaro del Portillo. Time and again, St Josemaría would recall years later, Alvaro was ready to take on different tasks and was most efficient in sorting them out. The more St Josemaría entrusted him with, he discovered, the more he could rely on him.

The Founder of Opus Dei said that, at the beginning, he hadn't thought of Blessed Alvaro as the one who could share his burden but, in very descriptive words, St Josemaría said, he "*found him.*" Alvaro was there. He was always there. When the Founder needed anything, Blessed Alvaro was ready and always accepted.

Like that diligent child with several siblings who found herself fed up of being asked all the time to do chores at home. When she couldn't take it anymore, she complained to her mother, "*Why do you always ask me to do everything? Why don't you ask the others?"* Her mum, with a smile and holding her face in her hands, replied, *"Because I know **you** will do it."*

That is it. When a captain wants something done, he entrusts it to his best soldier. God does the same. When He wants something done He relies on those who have proved trustworthy. In other words, *"Whoever is faithful in a very little is faithful also in much."* God could rely on Mary because she was always ready to say 'Yes' to the big and to the small; to much and to little.

This raises the question for our personal examination: *'Am I reliable?'* Because if we are reliable in little things, then we are reliable in big things. If you are reliable in doing your mental prayer every day, in offering up little sacrifices, in starting your study on time, in finishing your work on time, in paying attention in class, in being patient with that person who is more challenging, in tidying your room, in doing your chores, in keeping your appointments – in a nutshell, in doing what you ought to do… then you can be asked to do more.

Our Lady was blessed because she heard the Word of God and kept It, because she was faithful in the little things first, because all she wanted was to do the Will of God. She proved reliable and so God could ask her for more.

Mary, Virgin Most Faithful, help me to be able to hear the Word of God, to listen to Him, to know His Will in my everyday life, to always say 'Yes' to everything, to be reliable; to be ready.

41

To be with Him

> *Jesus went up into the hills, and called to him those whom he desired; and they came to him. And he appointed twelve, to be with him, and to be sent out to preach and have authority to cast out demons* (Mk 3:13-15).

By then, Jesus had become famous. As we read earlier in the same chapter of St Mark, "*a great multitude from Galilee followed him; hearing all that he was doing, they came to him in great numbers from Judea, Jerusalem, Idumea, beyond the Jordan, and the region around Tyre and Sidon*" (Mk 3:7-8). Our Lord was able to select His Apostles from a large crowd. He knew them well. As St John explains, Jesus "*knew all people and needed no one to testify about anyone; for he himself knew what was in everyone*" (Jn 2:24-25).

That day Our Lord went up into the hills with His disciples. Some probably didn't follow Jesus uphill and stayed put. Still, a good number of people followed the Lord to the summit. Once there, we are told that Jesus "*called to him those whom he desired.*" That's what vocation is: God calling to Him those He wants. Maybe some of them wondered, *'Why me and not him or her?'* Others thought the opposite: *'Why Peter and not me?'* But it was pointless to search for a reason or an explanation. The reason was simple: Jesus wanted those and not others.

However, what we meditate on today is not the fact of the election of the Apostles, but the mission they were appointed for. The terms in the text are precise: Those twelve were called, not to be sent out immediately, not to teach others, contact other people, reach out to new villages... They were "*called to Him,*" the text says. The essence of the calling of the Apostles wasn't to '**do**' something. It was to '**be**' with Jesus.

More often than not, when people consider the possible vocations God may want for them, they think of a mission, '*something I have to do*'. Instead, St Mark explains in his Gospel, the essence of a vocation is not about doing something, carrying out a mission, but about being with Jesus. The Scripture is clear about it: Jesus "*appointed twelve, to be with him.*"

So when they asked Jesus, '*OK now, Jesus, what do we have to do?*' Jesus could well reply, '*Be with Me.*'

Whatever vocation we may have, be it to become a nun, a monk, a friar, a priest, a mum, a dad, a deacon, a celibate apostle in the middle of the world or a missionary in Siberia, it makes no difference. We are called to be with Him. That was the main point about the twelve Apostles. They would be, of course, "*sent out to preach and have authority to cast out demons*"; they would go to the whole world, spread the Gospel of the Lord, convert many, preach everywhere, heal many, be persecuted and die for Jesus... But that could only be possible because '*they were with Jesus.*'

To be with Him is the essence of any vocation. And since we know we have a vocation, we know an 'essential' part of it: whatever vocation it is, we are called to be with Jesus. When we take this to our prayer we need to ask ourselves honestly: "Lord, how close am I to You?... Am I with You?"

A classic term used to express the idea of being with Jesus is *'contemplation.'* A contemplative soul is in the presence of God all the time. Whatever she does, that soul keeps the countenance of her beloved in front of her. A contemplative soul can be cooking, sweeping, cleaning, running, shopping, eating, studying or driving and still *"be with Him."* That is possible because from the beginning, they were with Him. Like the Apostles, before they could be sent out and entrusted missions, they needed *"to be with Him."*

The gist of this chapter is: "Before action, we need contemplation." There is no action if there is no contemplation. In fact, contemplation is the fuel for action. Contemplation is action.

Fr Willie Doyle was an Irish Jesuit priest who was killed in action during the First World War. As a military chaplain he was renowned for his courage. He was presented with the *parchment of merit* of the 49th (Irish) Brigade. He was killed in the Battle of Langemarck on 16 August 1917. *"He went forward and back over the battlefield,"* reads an article in *The Morning Post*, *"with bullets whining about him, seeking out the dying and kneeling in the mud beside them to give them Absolution, walking with death with a smile on his face, watched by his men with reverence and a kind of awe... His familiar figure was seen and welcomed by hundreds of Irishmen who lay in that bloody place. Each time he came back across the field he was begged to remain in comparative safety. Smilingly he shook his head and went again into the storm...They remember him as a saint - they speak his name in tears"* (Percival Phillips in The Morning Post, 22nd August 1917).

General Hickie, the commander-in-chief of the 16th (Irish) Division, described Doyle as *"one of the bravest men who fought or served out here."* In a letter to Doyle's parents he wrote: *"I could not say too much about your son. He was loved and reverenced by all of us; his gallantry, self-sacrifice, and devotion to duty were all so well known and recognized. I think that his was the most wonderful character that I have ever known."*

When, after his death, they collected his notes and letters, they discovered the fuel that kept him in action. His life of prayer was intense. He prayed during the day and during the night. He celebrated Mass wherever he could. He loved God and his people and risked his life thousands of times to bring them together until a shell burst near him and killed him. There's no action without contemplation…

Among his notes, Fr Willie Doyle left written: "*I have long had the feeling that, since the world is growing so rapidly worse and worse and God has lost His hold, as it were, upon the hearts of men, He is looking all the more earnestly and anxiously for big things from those who are faithful to Him still. He cannot, perhaps, gather a large army around His standard, but He wants everyone in it to be a Hero, absolutely and lovingly devoted to Him; if only we could get inside that magic circle of generous souls, I believe there is no grace He would not give us to help the work He has so much at heart, our personal sanctification. Every day means an infallible growth in holiness which may be multiplied a thousand times by a little generosity… holiness means three things: - Love, Prayer, Sacrifice.*"

Mary, Help of Christians, help me to grow in prayer (true contemplative life) to be able to '*be with your Son always.*'

42

Just by chance?

> *So he came to a city of Samaria, called Sychar, near the field that Jacob gave to his son Joseph. Jacob's well was there, and so Jesus, wearied as he was with his journey, sat down beside the well. It was about the sixth hour. There came a woman of Samaria to draw water. Jesus said to her, "Give me a drink." For his disciples had gone away into the city to buy food. The Samaritan woman said to him, "How is it that you, a Jew, ask a drink of me, a woman of Samaria?"* (Jn 4:5-9).

That woman went for water at about the sixth hour. Coincidentally, Jesus was in the exact same place at the exact same time. Just by chance, His disciples had gone to the city to get something to eat. Incidentally, nobody else was there to interrupt the conversation. It all happened as if *by chance*. But did it?

Of course not. God had prepared that moment with care for millions of centuries. God wanted to meet that lady, that day, at that place, to open her heart and use her as an instrument to reach out to all the people in her village. We remember the scene well. After a few sentences, the lady realised that the Man in front of her was a special Person. *"I perceive that you are a prophet,"* she said.

Once the disciples were back, the woman ran back into the village. In her haste, she even left her water jar behind. She then invited the people to go and meet Jesus in person: "*They went out of the city and were coming to him*" (Jn 4:30). In the end, many of those Samaritans believed in Our Lord: "*It is no longer because of your words that we believe,*" they said to the woman, "*for we have heard for ourselves, and we know that this is indeed the Saviour of the world.*"

A great crowd believed in Jesus that day, seemingly as a result of a casual encounter between Our Lord and the woman. The truth is instead quite different. For God there is no coincidence or chance; there is only Providence.

In August 1930, a young industrial engineer named Isidoro Zorzano was travelling from Malaga, where he lived at the time, to Madrid. He was to take a train to Logroño to spend his holidays there with his family. Since he had a bit of time until the train's departure, he decided to take a short walk through the streets of Madrid. He tried to visit an old school friend, St Josemaría Escrivá, but couldn't find him because the priest wasn't in the church where he worked.

That very day, St Josemaría Escrivá was visiting a sick person. "*All of a sudden,*" St Josemaría explained years later, "*I felt a bit uneasy and decided to leave earlier than normal.*" They tried to dissuade him from leaving and invited the priest for lunch, but he declined. He didn't know why, but he felt he had to leave. Once in the street, he decided to take a different route than usual to get back home. Suddenly, just around the corner, he found himself in front of his old school friend, Isidoro. They hadn't met for years and St Josemaría didn't know he was in Madrid on his way to Logroño.

After the initial moment of confusion and surprise, they chatted for a while and Isidoro told his priest friend about his life. He explained his uneasiness at the possibility that God might be asking something from him. St Josemaría explained to him what Opus Dei was: the institution he had founded less than two years before. Isidoro listened carefully, asked questions, reflected, and decided to take a break to pray about it. He went to a church to pray. There, in dialogue with God, he saw the Hand of Divine Providence behind this seemingly fortuitous encounter, behind his doubts and feelings of uneasiness. He understood everything was clearly designed by God. From that day on, he had total confidence in his vocation as a numerary in Opus Dei and he was a model of faithfulness to his calling until he died, in 1943, with a reputation for sanctity. Recognised today as Venerable Isidoro Zorzano, he could easily have dismissed his vocation, claiming that the encounter with St Josemaría had been just a trivial coincidence. But he knew that *God's Providence takes no chances*.

In 1588, a young Neapolitan man called Ascanio Caracciolo received a letter from Agostino Adorno, seeking advice about starting a new religious community and asking him for cooperation. The funny thing was that the letter he read wasn't addressed to him. It was sent to a relative of his who happened to have the same name. How strange is that? Nevertheless, the young lad understood that it was the precise Will of God and he decided to join the new Clerics Regular Minor order. Well, he didn't just join: he became co-founder and he is known today as Saint Francis Caracciolo.

How easily St Francis could have discarded the possibility that God was calling him by sending a letter to someone else! But he also knew that *God's Providence takes no chances*.

It is not by chance that St. Maximilian Kolbe heard during a homily in 1906 the news that a new Franciscan seminary was opening in Lvov and he would decide to enter there a few months later. It wasn't coincidental that St John of God was in Granada in 1539 listening to the preaching of St John of Ávila and that this made him change his life completely. It wasn't a coincidence that St Camillus de Lellis had to go to St James' Hospital in Rome in 1582 to treat a wound and discovered there his mission to begin a congregation dedicated to the care of the sick.

It wasn't by chance that Jesus met the Samaritan woman by the well on that day, at that precise time. It wasn't by chance that Jesus passed by when St John the Baptist was with his two disciples, Andrew and John, so that the Baptist would invite them to follow Our Lord. It wasn't by chance that Jesus walked by the Sea of Galilee when the fishermen were tidying up, or when He entered St Matthew's tax office, or when He mentioned to Nathanael that He saw him under a particular fig tree...

Let's take a look at our lives, remembering that God has been accompanying us all the way, every single step of it. He has surrounded us with the very people who had to share the important moments of our life with us. If we had discarded something as a meaningless coincidence, we may want to think again and remember that *God takes no chances.* As St Paul taught the Romans: "*We know that all things work together for good for those who love God, who are called according to his purpose*" (8:28). Everything works for our good. Everything is according to God's purpose.

Mary, Mother of Good Counsel, help me to see the Hand of God behind the seemingly 'chance' moments of my life.

43

Waiting for a signal.

> *The next day John was standing with two of his disciples; and he looked at Jesus as he walked, and said, "Behold, the Lamb of God!" The two disciples heard him say this, and they followed Jesus. Jesus turned, and saw them following, and said to them, "What do you seek?" And they said to him, "Rabbi" (which means Teacher), "where are you staying?" He said to them, "Come and see." They came and saw where he was staying; and they stayed with him that day, for it was about the tenth hour. One of the two who heard John speak, and followed him, was Andrew, Simon Peter's brother. He first found his brother Simon, and said to him, "We have found the Messiah" (which means Christ). He brought him to Jesus. Jesus looked at him, and said, "So you are Simon the son of John? You shall be called Cephas" (Jn 1:35-42).*

The calling of the first disciples of Jesus couldn't be more anticlimactic. When John and Andrew started following Jesus, all they knew was that John the Baptist said He was the Lamb of God. They stayed with Our Lord one day and then the next and the next – and for the rest of their lives.

Next thing we know is that one day Jesus passed by the Sea of Galilee and saw Peter and Andrew *"casting a net into the lake, for they were fishermen."* So Our Lord said to them, *"Come, follow me and I will send you out to fish for people."* And *"at once"* explains St Matthew, *"they left their nets and followed him"* (Mt 4:18-20).

The quote from St John's Gospel that opens this chapter continues saying that *"the next day Jesus decided to go to Galilee. And he found Philip and said to him, 'Follow me'"* (Jn 1:43). And that was it.

St Matthew describes his own calling with these words: *"As Jesus passed on from there, he saw a man called Matthew sitting at the tax office; and he said to him, 'Follow me.' And he rose and followed him"* (Mt 9:9). That's it.

All these accounts share the same simplicity. If these were scripts for a movie or lines of an autobiography, they would never work. You can imagine the audience or the reader thinking, *"What? That's it?! ... Just like that?!"* I'm afraid so.

In our modern-day world, we are used to seeing high drama, sensational special effects, romantic moments, shining colours, beautiful backgrounds, stunning soundtracks and lighting effects. But *life is not a movie.* If we had written the script we could have included the raising of a dead man, the healing of a paralytic which startle the disciples – and then Jesus says something like, *'If you want to see more of that, come and follow me!'*

Yes, Jesus could have convinced them with some miracles. He could have performed some signs before the calling, read their minds, prophesied something or moved the shade of a tree to impress the Apostles. He could have, indeed. However, He did nothing of the sort. This is the point: the Apostles didn't start following Jesus because they saw signs. *They saw signs after they started following Jesus.*

If fact, those who came to Jesus asking for signs went away without any. Jesus invariably told them that there were no more signs than those that had already been performed – and if those were not enough for them, no other sign would work anyway. Jesus explained this point in the parable of Lazarus and the rich man (*Lk* 16:19-31). When the rich man asks Abraham to send Lazarus to visit his relatives and warn them about the existence of hell, Abraham replies, "*They have Moses and the Prophets; let them listen to them.*" The rich man insists, "*No, father Abraham... but if someone from the dead goes to them, they will repent.*" To which Abraham retorts emphatically, "*If they do not listen to Moses and the Prophets, they will not be convinced even if someone rises from the dead.*" Nothing would be a sufficiently significant sign for them.

Many people spend their lives waiting for a special sign. They may think that just because Gabriel visited Mary, he may as well be free today, pop by and also tell them something. We shouldn't expect the extraordinary when the ordinary will do. "*Looked at this way,*" writes Jose Luis Soria, "*a vocation might be compared to God's action in the Incarnation or the Eucharist, making all due allowance for the difference in the greatness of the things considered. In the Incarnation God became Man and, to those who did not have the eyes of faith and a clean heart, it seemed that he was nothing more than a man (ref. Mt 16:13-17). In the Eucharist there seems to be nothing but bread and yet God is there, really present, Body and Blood, Soul and Divinity. A vocation is God's voice calling us, but usually under cover of the daily events, or the people we meet, or the circumstances we find ourselves in.*"

A young person described her vocation with these words: "I had been praying about vocation for a long time. One day I was reading the conversion of St Paul (*Acts* 22). Paul recovered his sight after Ananias laid his hands on him and then, the old man said, '*The God of our ancestors has chosen you to know his will and to see the Righteous One and to hear words from his mouth. You will be his witness to all people of what you have seen and heard. And now what are you waiting for? Get up'* (v 14-16). Those last words echoed in my mind for a while: *'What are you waiting for?'* Then I saw myself stuck for months, waiting, expecting a sign – a clear perception. *'Awaiting what?'* I didn't know. *'Well then,'* I thought, *'if I didn't know what to expect... how could I tell when it had arrived?'* And I understood. I knew all I had to know. I knew that God wanted me entirely for Himself and I knew *'I knew,'* but still expected a *'didn't-know-what-exactly'* to confirm what had been growing slowly in my soul. The ball had been in my court for a long time and I couldn't see it because I was looking around but not at my feet. I had *God* waiting when I thought He had *me* waiting. The echo kept ringing in my heart: "*What are you waiting for? Get up!*" So I got up and said *'Yes'*."

When considering our vocation, we should focus more on the very ordinary events, the people God has put in my life... We will also consider, of course, some extraordinary events that happen in everyone's life. Some saints had singular turning points at a particular moment of their lives. Still, the discovery of their vocation didn't happen in an instant but after a slow process of deliberation: prayer, sacraments, spiritual guidance, reading...

Most of the saints never received a visit from St Gabriel, or any angel or any saint. They never saw anything extraordinary in their lives. Yet, when they died, people found that the single extraordinary thing about them is that *they themselves were extraordinary people.*

Jesus didn't impose Himself on His disciples with astonishing miracles. They saw miracles, of course. Many of them. Yet they didn't follow Jesus because of His miracles but because of His Love. Love is the sign that many are expecting to see. But "*ay, there's the rub!*" Love is invisible and yet... so evident!

Mary, Mother of Divine Grace, don't let me spend my life waiting for signs that will not come. Give me instead the light I need to recognise God speaking to me through the most ordinary events of my life.

44

Saints were not saints inevitably

> *There were many women there...who had followed Jesus from Galilee, ministering to him; among whom were Mary Magdalene, and Mary the mother of James and Joseph, and the mother of the sons of Zebedee (Mt 27:55-56).*

Those are the names mentioned by St Matthew of those who were at the foot of the Cross. St John adds Our Lady's sister and *Mary the wife of Clopas* (Jn 19:25-26). St Mark adds "*Salome, who, when he was in Galilee, followed him, and ministered to him; and also many other women who came up with him to Jerusalem*" (Mk 15:40-41). And St Luke also mentions Joseph of Arimathea (Lk 23:50).

It can be a bit confusing to realise that they may not be the ones we expected to find there. If, after reading the Gospels up to Holy Week, we were asked to write a list with the names of the people we thought we would find at Calvary, we would never have guessed correctly.

Our Lady, of course, could be a winner, and St John, and Mary Magdalene. But very likely, we are missing most of the other names that we would expect to see there. Where were Peter, James, Andrew... OK. They were hiding. But what about Zacchaeus, maybe? Wouldn't he want to be there? Or what about Bartimaeus or any of the paralytics or lepers; or the deaf, lame or possessed people who were healed by Jesus? What about the centurion? After having his servant healed... where is he?

Where is Lazarus? Where is the widow of Naim or Jairus, who saw their beloved children come back to life? Where is the Samaritan woman or any of the Samaritans who said they believed in Jesus? Where are those who ate loaves and fish galore, or drank the best wine at Cana?

And there's something else that strikes us: who is Mary's sister? Who are all the other Marys, the mother of James and Joseph, the wife of Clopas? Who is Salome? And who are the *"many other women"* that St Mark mentions? Who are these people?

Those we expected are not there. Those who are there... they are unknown to us. But Jesus expected them. They are anonymous for us but not for God. One of the clear ideas that we can get from the Gospels is that, many times, those who looked promising didn't do much and those you least expected took on more relevance in early Christianity.

The rich young man looked like a talented asset. Nevertheless, he ended up being a flop. Mary Magdalene, on the other hand, probably wasn't that promising at the beginning – and yet we owe her so much. However, let's understand this well. It is not that God assigned to some people main roles in His play, whilst others were offered just a few lines as compensation. No. God assigned great roles to everyone. Everyone was meant to become a *main character* from the beginning. But not everyone accepted.

We get the clear and distinct idea that saints are not people who were inexorably or unstoppably holy. Just like sinners were not inevitably weak. It may elicit feelings of relief and comfort to think that God especially tailored saints for holiness whilst we are just *average* children of God. It may, of course, be enunciated in many different ways, but the idea remains in the back of the minds of many Christians: those saints whose lives we read in books were somehow given a particular advantage.

That wouldn't be fair. It would be like a race where a few runners are given a head start before the rest can begin the run. It is still a dumb device to justify ourselves and appease our conscience. '*If I am not like St Francis of Assisi,*' we could think, '*it is because he was special and I am not.*'

Those people we see with special talents may be like a large seed. The size of the tree is never measured by the size of the seed. A brilliant, magnificent, large seed can be planted in a small pot and produce a ridiculous bonsai. Because if the roots don't grow downwards, the tree doesn't grow upwards. Thus, many talented Christians have limited the growth of their roots so that they can only live a '*bonsai-sized*' Christian life now.

Following the quote from the Gospel that opens this chapter, we could say that every vocation is a climb up to Calvary. We all have what it takes to reach the summit. Those who were there on Good Friday were in love with Jesus and had the courage to climb up with Him. The others, those who didn't show up on that day, would, in their turn, climb up to Golgotha on another day; Peter, James, Andrew and Philip did climb to Calvary later, and so did Paul and Timothy and Titus, Agnes and Felicity, Augustine and Justin and Patrick and Thomas More and Edith Stein... and so will you and I.

We are all called, by divine vocation, to accompany Jesus in His Passion and Death, because only in that way will we also have a share in His Resurrection. All of us have a choice. Just as Mary Magdalene could have stayed at home that day, or John could have joined the other Apostles in their hiding place, St

Francis had the choice to lead an easy life, St Thomas More and John Fisher had the choice to take an oath and save their necks, and every saint of the calendar could have chosen to lead an average, easy Christian life – a life in the coop.

There were people watching Jesus die from a distance. Everyone could choose the distance they wanted to be at. But we have no names, no remembrance of those. Only the names of the people who were in the front line, next to Our Lord; only those Jesus could see from the Cross; only those who loved Him so much, they didn't care what could happen to them.

The point is simple. Whatever vocation you have, it is not an *'average'* vocation or a call to an *'average'* Christian life. There is no average holiness. Holiness is always heroic. To be average is to be mediocre – and that is incompatible with holiness.

Many well-intentioned, talented, high-profile people who were called to the same holiness didn't climb up to Calvary. However, there is a numerous army of discrete, averagely talented, apparently irrelevant souls who reach the summit of Calvary in silence, without display, under the radar. Souls who would never attract people's attention; they only attract God's grace. Souls who love Jesus Christ and never think about themselves. Souls who have their eyes set on Our Lord and whose only concern is to be close to Him, whatever it takes.

And the world is craving these souls: saints below the radar, discrete *Frodo-Baggins's-of-holiness*, who can walk under the very nose of the enemy unnoticed because there is no display, no external sign. And just as the seed grows in silence, so too, the Kingdom of God is growing without spectacle, slowly but constantly; unstoppable, relentless, at the pace of God and of those humble souls who say 'Yes' to Him.

Mary, Virgin Most Renowned, with your help, may I accompany you to the top of Golgotha, at the pace your Son is asking of me, generously, not dragging behind, not slowing down, not growing tired; and there, from the top of Calvary, open my wings to the wind of the Holy Spirit and fly high. Mary, my Mother, I ask you this particular grace: may I never get tired of climbing, may I never give up!

45

Expect opposition

> *Peter was sitting outside in the courtyard. And a maid came up to him, and said, "You also were with Jesus the Galilean." But he denied it before them all, saying, "I do not know what you mean." And when he went out to the porch, another maid saw him, and she said to the bystanders, "This man was with Jesus of Nazareth." And again he denied it with an oath, "I do not know the man." After a little while the bystanders came up and said to Peter, "Certainly you are also one of them, for your accent betrays you." Then he began to invoke a curse on himself and to swear, "I do not know the man." And immediately the cock crowed. And Peter remembered the saying of Jesus, "Before the cock crows, you will deny me three times." And he went out and wept bitterly* (Mt 26:69-75).

Those who have decided to say 'Yes' and follow God should expect opposition. They have voluntarily moved to the front line of battle and the enemy is relentless against them. The following testimony of a young priest could help us to describe this point. I use it with his permission, intentionally guarding his anonymity as he requested:

"Ever since my teenage years I could feel God was asking something big of me. I used to attend means of formation in an Opus Dei centre. There and at home, I was imbued with the certainty that accepting my vocation would always be the best option. I became a young numerary candidate at the age of 15 and spent my teens struggling to keep up with my plan of life - life of prayer, daily Mass, frequent confession, regular spiritual guidance...

"At university, fidelity to my celibate vocation was challenged a few times but with God's grace and the help of my spiritual director, every fire was conveniently put out. The day came when it was suggested to me to study theology in Rome and I accepted. During those five years I spent in the Eternal City, it was like a honeymoon with my vocation. At the end of that period of study, I was asked if I would like to become a priest and I said 'Yes'.

"Then the storm broke out - a spiritual typhoon.

"Suddenly I started suffering temptations I hadn't felt since I was thirteen. I was confused by the intensity of those temptations. I was bewildered by the persistence of those trials: horrible temptations against chastity, against obedience, against charity. Most of them absolutely new to me or felt in a way I had never experienced in my life. In the midst of that turmoil, I kept asking God 'Why?' - trying to find the cause, the origin of this trial.

"A series of thoughts started haunting me: 'Was it my fault?', 'Did I do something wrong?' 'Was God upset with me?' But the question that most tortured my heart was: 'Should I become a priest?', 'Should I give up?', or even 'Am I the right person?', 'Can I become a priest?'

"In this state of mind I went to talk to the spiritual director and opened my soul to him. I asked him if I should renounce my ordination given the circumstances. The priest listened to me with a serene smile. When I finished he smiled openly and repeated a well-known line from a film we both enjoyed very much: "Welcome to the party, pal!"

"The words come from John McLain (Bruce Willis), in 'Die Hard', when the policeman suddenly finds himself caught in the middle of the battle.

"The priest continued explaining how, when a soul decides to give himself up to God, the enemy always deploys a ferocious attack. The experience is well known. Souls who advance to the front of the battle will always feel the enemy's fury. He hates generous souls, committed souls, chosen souls who accept the challenge. They are his main enemies and so he fights with all his might."

Thus, whenever a soul has to face a new stage, when important decisions have to be made, when a leap in generosity, a new commitment, a conversion is coming up, **expect opposition!**

'*Your mission, should you accept it,*' will always attract the enemy's attention. The devil will mess about, he will try, he will persist, he will not give up and will give us hard moments. When those times come, all we need to know is that we may be doing well if the enemy is so furious with us. It will be an indirect confirmation that our *artillery* is hitting the enemy's position. We are on target. Let's keep it up!

In 1910 young seminarian Maximillian was facing an important decision. He had to make up his mind if he wanted to be ordained a priest. For a long time he had it clear, but when the moment got closer, doubts started to arise. After thinking about it, he made up his mind to leave the seminary. One day he received an unexpected visit from his mother and decided to explain to her his doubts and his decision. However, before he could mention anything, his mother started talking with great enthusiasm about the vocations of Maximillian's siblings. That encounter reassured him and he decided to keep going with his vocation. So he did, thank goodness, because otherwise we wouldn't have the example of St Maximillian Kolbe.

In 1921, after a year in the seminary, Josemaría left Saragossa to join his family during the summer holidays. The year had been hard for him. Years later he mentioned that *"many hard things, terrible things"* happened there. He described them as *"axe blows."* During the summer he decided he wouldn't go back to the seminary for the beginning of the new academic year. However, after a conversation with a priest in Logroño, he decided to do otherwise and did re-join the seminary in September. *"Where would I be now"*, he prayed out loud years later, *"had You not prevented my leaving the seminary of Saragossa when I believed I had mistaken my path...?"* And where would many thousands of other people be, we wonder, had St Josemaría not re-joined the seminary to become a priest and a saint?

In 1935, a year before the Spanish Civil War broke out, a young engineering student, Jose Maria, joined Opus Dei. He spent most of the war in prison, constantly under threat of death. This isolation didn't help his vocation much. He lost contact with other members of the Work and felt doubts about his calling. When the war finished, he made up his mind to meet St Josemaría to let him know his intention to leave Opus Dei. But when he went to the centre where St Josemaría was at the time in Madrid, he met lots of other members of the Work who greeted him with such affection and enthusiasm, that it made him waver and reconsider the step he was about to take.

In fact, he never did take that step. Instead, he threw himself into living his vocation to the full. Years later he became one of the first three priests of Opus Dei, and eventually helped to expand the Work in the USA, Mexico, Guatemala, Venezuela, Colombia, Ecuador, Peru, Chile, Argentina, UK, Ireland, France, Germany, Austria, Belgium, the Netherlands and Switzerland. Servant of God Jose Maria Hernandez Garnica died in 1972 with a reputation for holiness and his cause for canonization is in progress today.

Considering these cases and thousands more that could be brought to our meditation, we understand well why they faced opposition in those defining moments of their lives: the enemy hated them. The tempter knew he had to do something; he probably tried his best. But thanks be to God, his best wasn't enough and they were faithful.

The denial of St Peter opened this chapter. Another brilliant example of a saint who knew how to pick himself up – or better, to let God pick him up – and do what Our Lord needed him to do.

Mary, Mother Most Faithful, help me and all those Christians who face opposition today and are tempted to turn their backs on their vocation; with your intercession, my Mother, may I always react with generosity when those defining moments come in my life.

46

In the thick of it

> *As he sat at table in the house, behold, many tax collectors and sinners came and sat down with Jesus and his disciples. And when the Pharisees saw this, they said to his disciples, "Why does your teacher eat with tax collectors and sinners?" But when he heard it, he said, "Those who are well have no need of a physician, but those who are sick. Go and learn what this means, 'I desire mercy, and not sacrifice.' For I came not to call the righteous, but sinners."* (Mt 9:10-13)

We are familiar with the constant criticisms of the Pharisees against Jesus: He mingled with impure people. The very word 'Pharisee' comes from the Aramaic *'perisayya'*, which means *'separated'*. According to the Law given by God to Moses, the Jews could contaminate themselves through contact with *unclean* people. Thus, if they touched a non-Jewish person, a dead body or blood, lepers, impure animals, or any sinner for that matter, they had to undergo a process of purification. Because of the corruption of many of the People of Israel, it was increasingly difficult to keep themselves pure. To ensure their cleanliness, the Pharisees had decided to 'separate' themselves from them.

Thus, Pharisees would never deal with non-Jews or sinners; they didn't get anywhere near lepers, bleeding people, in fact, any sick person in general, just in case... As we can see, the number of people they could actually deal with was significantly reduced. But they didn't care. That's why they were Pharisees – '*separated*'.

However, for them there was something especially annoying about Jesus. Instead of He Himself becoming impure, when He touched impure people, He didn't lose His purity, *He* purified *them*! Jesus' purity was such that He would touch a bleeding lady and, instead of becoming impure, He would heal that lady's 'impurity' – her bleeding. Jesus would touch lepers and remove their 'impurity' – their leprosy. Jesus Christ is the source of purity and can purify impurity with His touch without losing any bit of purity Himself.

The Pharisees were jealous. They couldn't do that. They didn't have the purity it took to *purify impurity* just by touching it. That took extraordinary purity, and they didn't have it. If they touched impurity they got stained. So all they could do is, again, to remain separated.

There are some Christians who are called by God to purify the world with their touch without getting stained. It is the most difficult vocation. Here is why: It's more difficult to live temperance when you have a buffet breakfast with no limits than when all you have is a cheese sandwich. It's more difficult to live detachment from material things when you have a credit card in your pocket with unlimited funds than when all you have fits in a backpack. It's more challenging to abstain from alcoholic drinks when you work in a distillery than when you don't have access to alcohol at all.

There are vocations by which God calls His children to withdraw from the world, to live in a monastery or in a convent and there, away from distractions and other worries, dedicate all their energies to prayer, work and contemplation. It has its own challenges that are very different from the challenge of sanctifying the world in the midst of it.

It is a real challenge to live poverty and detachment when you have access to anything, to live temperance when you have your table full of food, your fridge packed, your Wi-Fi at high speed and 5G data on your phone. It is a challenge to live Holy Purity when every other website on the internet offers you an impure option, when any film, Netflix series or TV programme threatens to show you, out of the blue, more contents than you want to see or when immodest people show too much of themselves in the streets, at college or on public transport.

That's the reality of those who have the vocation to sanctify the world from the inside: those who have to live the *truth* in a *dishonest* world, *charity* in the middle of *hatred*, *generosity* in a *selfish* environment, *humility* in a world of *vanity*, *purity* in an *immoral* society, *temperance* in the paradise of *abundance*, *peace* in social *turmoil*, *joy* in a sea of *misery*, *hope* amongst the *hopeless* and *faith* amongst the *faithless*...

It takes a very pure heart to be in the thick of it and still keep yourself pure. It takes a lot of grace to touch all that and not to get stained with it. And that is precisely the place where Jesus wants most of His disciples. He was praying to the Father during the Last Supper: *"I do not pray that thou shouldst take them out of the world, but that thou shouldst keep them from the evil one"* (*Jn* 17:15).

Our Lord warned us in many ways that we would be at war here: *"From the days of John the Baptist until now the kingdom of heaven has suffered violence, and men of violence take it by force"* (*Mt* 11:12). *"Militia est vita hominis super terram"*, says the Book of Job (7:1), which can be translated, *"a man's life is warfare."* However,

Jesus didn't ask His disciples to step back, but to face adversity with confidence: *"In the world you have tribulation; but be of good cheer, I have overcome the world"* (Jn 16:33).

In every war there are soldiers in many different positions, all of them necessary to the victory. It is vital, then, when praying about vocation, to find out what my position is in this army of peace to set the Kingdom of God on earth.

A small proportion of the army is in the rear-guard. They keep the chain of command, they process the intelligence reports, transmit information, liaise with allies, coordinate strategy, organise the provision of food and medicine and the supplies of ammunition, weapons and reinforcements. They are vital and absolutely necessary.

But still the majority of the armed forces are on the front line. Usually, they are the ones who shoot and take the shots, the ones who dodge the enemy's artillery, those who hold the front line, who get wounded, who are hungry and thirsty and exhausted most of the time, or die in the line of duty. For all that, they need to be fit, to train their skills, their shot, their resilience; they need to trust their superiors, follow commands and interpret orders; they have to rely on the suppliers, to keep pressing, to persevere in the same position or to scout behind enemy lines, to patrol uncharted territory, to dig the trenches that will protect those who come behind; they are the ones who earn the victory.

The army of the Kingdom of God needs vocations in all positions. Contemplative vocations, in the rear-guard, get the vital supply to the rest of the army (prayer, sacrifice, work... i.e. food, ammunition, support). We need many of those. But the vocation of those Christians who are in the middle of the world (celibate or married, consecrated or not) is of critical importance since they constitute the majority of the army. They need to get fit for this battle to be able to step on the battlefield without getting stained by it, to purify the world without losing their purity.

The war to establish the Kingdom of God needs *everything everyone* can give. Whatever vocation you have, whatever your position in this battlefield, find it out, *check the draft* in your prayer because by now we have taken too many casualties and are in dire need of your holiness – all of it!

Mary, my Mother, Queen of the Universe, Help of Christians, lead your children in this battle against the beast whose head has been crushed (*Rev* 12:17); assist your children and guide us, Mother, Star of the Sea, so that we all find our place in this battlefield, are faithful to our mission, keep our position, defend our ground and conquer for your Son, King of the Universe, the parts of this world that still do not submit to Him.

47

The Disciple Jesus Loved

> *The next day John again was standing with two of his disciples, and as he watched Jesus walk by, he exclaimed, 'Look, here is the Lamb of God!' The two disciples heard him say this, and they followed Jesus. When Jesus turned and saw them following, he said to them, 'What are you looking for?' They said to him, 'Rabbi' (which translated means Teacher), 'where are you staying?' He said to them, 'Come and see.' They came and saw where he was staying, and they remained with him that day. It was about four o'clock in the afternoon (Jn 1:35-39).*

John was a young lad when he first met Jesus. Tradition suggests he was about 14 when he followed St John the Baptist who was preaching by the banks of the Jordan, preparing for the imminent arrival of the Lord. The words of the Precursor stirred up the young man's desires to see the Messiah. One day they saw Jesus passing by and the Baptist sent his young disciples to Him. As we read, Andrew and John followed Our Lord, spent that day with Him – and every day for the rest of their lives. When the Beloved Disciple wrote his Gospel (at about 90 years old), he had in his mind clear memories of every detail lived with Jesus. He remembered perfectly the time that the Lord crossed his path: "*It was about four o'clock in the afternoon.*"

John was from Bethsaida, a city of Galilee, on the northern shore of the Lake of Tiberius. His parents were Zebedee and Salome; James was his older brother. They were a wealthy family of fishermen. One day Jesus passed by the Lake of Tiberius and found James and John with their father. Up until that day, John had been following Jesus and listening to Him at times, but he still kept up with his duties. However, on that day Our Lord called James and John to follow Him 'full-time'.

From that day on John would accompany Jesus everywhere. After a while, the young lad came to the realisation that Our Lord loved him and John started feeling that he was "*the Disciple Whom Jesus Loved*". Then he started growing fond of Jesus and loving Him as he had never loved anybody else in his short life.

John had a powerful character and his impulsive reactions revealed some traces of ambition, impatience and pride. On one occasion, the disciples saw someone casting out devils using the Name of Jesus, without being a 'member' of the group. John said to Jesus: "*Master, we saw someone casting out demons in your name, and we tried to stop him, because he does not follow with us*" (Lk 9:49). Jesus had to correct him – anyone working for the Kingdom of God had to be allowed to do so. On another day, when the Samaritans of a particular village didn't want to receive Jesus, John and James suggested, "*Lord, do you want us to command fire to come down from heaven and consume them?*" (Lk 9:54). John wasn't perfect. But his daily interaction with Our Lord allowed Jesus to transform the character of that young disciple into the kind of personality needed for his mission.

How much John changed in those years with Jesus!

He also became part of the select group of disciples that were allowed to accompany Jesus on very particular occasions. With

Peter and James, he was a witness to the resurrection of the daughter of Jairus and to the Transfiguration of Our Lord. But very specially, the three of them were called to comfort Jesus during His Agony in the Garden of Gethsemane.

John was granted another gift that other disciples didn't receive. He was called to a celibate life, early in his youth. He lived Holy Purity from his early years, giving Jesus his undivided, exclusive and chaste heart. He could then love Our Lord with an intensity that not many can understand. As Jesus once said to His disciples, "*Not everyone can accept this teaching, but only those to whom it is given*" (*Mt* 19:11). To John it was given – and he understood it well.

Perhaps it was because of this complete and pure self-giving that he alone rested his head with confidence on the bosom of Our Lord during the Last Supper. What a graphic picture of the intimacy between John and Jesus! Perhaps he didn't say much but communicated his love to the Master, in those moments leading up to His Passion and Death – leaning on the side of Jesus that would be opened a few hours later, letting forth Blood and Water. So close to Jesus' Most Sacred Heart!

As we can see, John was special. He was the only Apostle to accompany Jesus during His ordeal. He was close to the Master during that Agony in Gethsemane. But he fell asleep. He didn't forget it: when Jesus needed him, John failed. He loved the Master, but he wasn't perfect. He had things to improve; just like you and me.

But John overcame that moment of weakness and later on, that same night, he accompanied Jesus to the courtyard of the high priest where He was being tried. He was there when the slaps and blows began, during the mockery, when they handed Jesus over to Pilate's palace to be judged by the governor. John was there during the scourging, the crowning of thorns. The young disciple accompanied Jesus through the streets of Jerusalem, as he carried the Cross; he climbed up to Calvary with Mary, following the slow, staggering steps of the Lord. John could never forget that day. Oh, what he witnessed, what he saw! So close to the Man he loved with his whole heart, Jesus, Who died in his presence in slow motion, killed by those merciless torturers, amid the shouting, the jeering, the insults and scorn of many; and contemplating the distress of Mary the Immaculate Mother together with the other women who followed Our Lord faithfully.

It was John who ran to the tomb before any other Apostle. It was he who let Peter enter first and see the place where Jesus' Body had been left. Among all the disciples who were with Peter fishing a few weeks later, it was John and no other who recognised Jesus in the distance. John it was who accompanied Peter to the temple, to preach, to perform miracles...

We wonder... Why was John so special? Why was it he who lived the events of Our Lord's Life more deeply than the others? What gave John such intimacy with Jesus, such love for Him? Why did Jesus seek out this young disciple for comfort? Why was John the one who rested his head on the Lord's chest? Where did he get the courage to witness Our Lord's Death so closely? We wonder... Why was John so special?

And above all, why was John the one to receive the sublime gift of Mary as a Mother for all Christians?

Was it not because he gave his whole youthful heart exclusively to Jesus? Because he accompanied Jesus everywhere? Because he never left the Master, he heard every single Word Jesus said with devotion, was humble enough to allow Jesus to correct him... because he tried to follow Our Lord's example? Was it not because of his chastity and purity of heart?

Some of the Fathers of the Church suggest that it was Holy Purity that made John suitable for the mission of caring for Our Lady. Jesus could entrust His *Virgin Mother* only to His *virgin disciple*. Let's pray about it: why could I not be "*the Disciple Jesus Loved*"? What is missing?

Mary, Mother of Christians, I ask through your intercession and through the intercession of St John, your beloved son, that I may imitate him in generosity, purity, courage, loyalty, faithfulness, devotion; and most of all in his love for you, my Mother, and undivided love for your Divine Son, Jesus.

48

Only one thing is necessary

> *Now as they went on their way, he entered a village; and a woman named Martha received him into her house. And she had a sister called Mary, who sat at the Lord's feet and listened to his teaching. But Martha was distracted with much serving; and she went to him and said, "Lord, do you not care that my sister has left me to serve alone? Tell her then to help me." But the Lord answered her, "Martha, Martha, you are anxious and troubled about many things; one thing is needful. Mary has chosen the good portion, which shall not be taken away from her"* (Lk 10:38-42).

You know the story. Jesus was in the house of His friends Lazarus, Martha and Mary. There was no better place for Jesus to stay when He was near Jerusalem. He felt at home there. That day Our Lord was teaching His disciples during the meal. But the problem was that the meal still had to be served, dishes had to be replaced, jugs had to be poured out, plates collected, cups refilled... Martha couldn't allow her Guest to lack anything on that occasion. However, her sister didn't feel the same way. Mary was, instead, listening to Jesus and paying no attention to anything else.

Martha's indignation grew every time she returned from the kitchen with another dish, a plate, or a cloth to wipe some spilled wine. There Mary was, indifferent to her sister's restlessness, absorbed by Jesus' words. When Martha tried to get her attention, Mary showed no interest in helping. For her, there was nobody else in that room but Jesus. Martha then attempted Plan B: She complained directly to Jesus, trying to get Him involved to convince Mary.

But it didn't work either. Jesus took Mary's side and reminded Martha that there are always many good things to do but, for that same reason, there is always one that is best. There are many things to be busy with but only one that's necessary. Only one thing matters: to stay with Jesus Christ.

Jesus' lesson to Martha does not *only* apply to activities that we can carry out in any particular moment, but also to our entire lives. The saints are those who never forgot that even though they could do many things with their talents, only one was necessary – to fulfil God's Will. Any other achievement in life, whatever it is, would be nothing compared to that. Let's meditate deeply on those words of Our Lord: "*For what will it profit them to gain the whole world and forfeit their life?*" (Mk 8:36).

The life of Blessed John Henry Newman is a good example of *getting our priorities right*. When he understood that his life was turning towards Catholicism, he could foresee some of the difficulties he would have to face, but could never imagine what his life was going to become. Muriel Spark, an English novelist and a convert himself, described Newman's autobiography, *Apologia pro Vita sua*, as "*the saddest love story in the world.*" He was rejected by Protestants and unwelcomed by Catholics. Even his family distanced themselves from him.

A few years after his conversion he wrote, "*O how forlorn and dreary has been my course since I have been a Catholic! Here has been the contrast – as a Protestant, I felt my religion dreary, but not my life – but, as a Catholic, my life dreary, not my religion ... Persons who would naturally look towards me, converts who would naturally come to me, inquirers who would naturally consult me, are stopped by some light or unkind word said against me."*

Many of his projects ended in failure. Newman ministered for long years after his conversion to a Catholic community that was unable, for the most part, to appreciate his special charisms and misinterpreted almost all his efforts. Later on he threw himself into establishing the Catholic University of Ireland, but the project failed because the bishops weren't ready. In 1854, Cardinal Wiseman wrote to announce that Bl Pius IX would name Newman bishop. Some friends sent him gifts (pectoral crosses, rings and mitre) but the ordination never happened because some bishops and priests wrote to Rome warning that the appointment was *imprudent*.

Shortly after, the English hierarchy commissioned Newman to work on a new English translation of the Bible and, after he had devoted a lot of effort to it, the project was cancelled. On another occasion, he was offered a large plot of land in Oxford and Newman enthusiastically drew up plans to develop a Catholic Centre for the university, staffed by priests who were former Oxford men. Again the plan was blocked by a group of Catholics.

Some prophets met the same fate. In particular, the life of the prophet Jeremiah is very similar. All the prophet's expectations went down the drain when the young king Josiah, who was to introduce some religious reforms, died in battle. Jeremiah was then afflicted with persecution from all sides, people (*Jer* 18:18), priests and false prophets (*Jer* 26). He was imprisoned and later accused of treason, sentenced to be thrown into the muddy bottom of an unused well where he almost starved to death (*Jer* 38:6-9). So overwhelmed by misfortune and finding no consolation, the Lord sent Jeremiah to comfort another prophet, Baruch! (*Jer* 45)

In one of his sermons, Cardinal Newman described the life of prophet Jeremiah with the words, *Great Hopes, Hard Works, Crushing Disappointments*. It isn't far from an autobiographical description. At the end of his life, Bl John Henry Newman died as a cardinal, but never became a bishop and left nothing but a few books.

Looked at from a human perspective, the life of Bl John Henry was a failure. With supernatural outlook though, the title of *Blessed* makes up for anything else since, as we have been meditating, only '*one thing is needed*' to become a saint. We must be ready to sacrifice any human projects we may have in order to subject them to the only purpose that matters.

"*Give not over your attempts to serve God,*" wrote Cardinal Newman, "*though you see nothing come of them. Watch and pray, and obey your conscience, though you cannot perceive your own progress in holiness. Go on, and you cannot but go forward; believe it, though you do not see it. Do the duties of your calling, though they are distasteful to you... Let your light shine before men, and praise God by a consistent life, even though others do not seem to glorify their Father on account of it, or to be benefited by your example.*"

Mary, Mother of Perpetual Help, help me to be true to my conscience and follow the path that your Son traces for me; I count on your assistance to be ready to subjugate all my human projects in favour of the divine one, the only one that matters.

49

Have you lost the star? Forwards!

> *Now when Jesus was born in Bethlehem of Judea in the days of Herod the king, behold, wise men from the East came to Jerusalem, saying, "Where is he who has been born king of the Jews? For we have seen his star in the East, and have come to worship him." When Herod the king heard this, he was troubled, and all Jerusalem with him... Then Herod sent them to Bethlehem...When they had heard the king they went their way; and lo, the star which they had seen in the East went before them, till it came to rest over the place where the child was. When they saw the star, they rejoiced exceedingly with great joy; and going into the house they saw the child with Mary his mother, and they fell down and worshiped him (Mt 2:1-3, 8-11).*

These Magi had travelled a long way following the star. It is believed that they were Zoroastrian priests who paid particular attention to the stars and recognised a particular one that was associated with the birth of the King of the Jews. These astrologers decided to leave their comfortable homes and travel all the way across the desert to find out what that star was revealing to them.

We don't know exactly where they came from. It is believed that they probably travelled from an area which is now in either Iraq, Iran, Saudi Arabia or the Yemen. All we know is that they came from the East. In any case, it was a long way and not an easy trek – it was across the desert. Tradition suggests there were three according to the three gifts they presented to Baby Jesus – gold, frankincense and myrrh.

We can guess that, if they had gold, they were probably wealthy (or at least reasonably well-off) in their countries of origin. They had to have the means to travel all the way through the desert with their own camels, servants and provisions for at least a few months, maybe years. They were certainly more comfortable in their own homes (or palaces) and didn't have to go anywhere.

Even more interesting is the fact that the expedition wasn't for business. They didn't expect to get anything from it. They would invest all it took to get there but didn't presume they'd be paid back, their expenses would be refunded or they'd get any economic compensation for their troubles. It wasn't in order to *get* anything. It was an investment to see the marvel (whatever it was) that the star was announcing.

It doesn't take much imagination to guess what their adventure was like. The desert is always the same: very hot during the day, very cold at night. There must have been some routes that ran from oasis to oasis but still they could spend days, maybe weeks, without a water supply. Under the sun, sweating, riding on the camels' humps, sand thrown in their faces by the hot breeze and getting into their eyes; having to find a spot to spend the night, pitch their tents, sleep on the floor; amidst windstorms, losing their way sometimes, unable to pinpoint the stars.

They didn't send their servants to see whether the star was actually proclaiming the birth of a king. They came themselves. They spared nothing in order to check for themselves the marvel of the new star. And after that long and uncomfortable trip across the desert, when their calculations suggested they were close to their destination, something very disturbing happened to them: the star disappeared. Just when they thought they were almost there, they lost the star!

Try to imagine what it was like. After all their troubles and painful progress through the desert; through the storms, the unknown villages, mountains and valleys; after all their toil, the star was nowhere to be found. So what did they do? Did they curse their bad luck and go back home? Did they doubt the accuracy of their past calculations? Did they waver in their determination to find out what exactly the new star was about? In a nutshell: did they give up? NO!

The determination that helped them go forwards was the certainty of what they had seen and not the uncertainty of what they couldn't see now. They didn't reinvent the past as if during their whole trip the star had been just a hallucination, a mind trick. The star was real. It had been real all the time. If they couldn't see the star it wasn't a problem with the skies. It was their problem. Maybe it was cloudy, maybe the star was aligned with another star, maybe it was an optical illusion... But they knew the star was real. They didn't hesitate: the star had been real for months and even years.

So they went and asked in Jerusalem. People seemed unconcerned about the birth of a new king and certainly indifferent to any change in the stars. Did they give up then? After all, nobody seemed to have seen their star. Perhaps it wasn't real after all. Did they stop there? NO!

Herod himself was summoned by these Magi to shed a bit of light on their confusion. And it was he (Herod, out of all the men on earth!) who put them back on track, pointing towards Bethlehem. *"When they had heard the king they went their way"*, says the Gospel; forwards again, towards a little village about six miles away. And it was then, after having walked on for days without sight of the star, after having asked for advice and directions and then setting off again and carrying on with their journey – without losing determination, without giving up, without stopping – that they saw what they were looking for.

"And lo," the Gospel of St Matthew continues, *"the star which they had seen in the East went before them."* The star again! It was there. It *was* real. It hadn't disappeared. It was they who couldn't see it. Now it was leading their way again and their doubts vanished.

The Gospel expresses their joy with very emphatic words: *"When they saw the star, they rejoiced exceedingly with great joy."* It sounds exaggerated, but this is a very accurate translation of the words that we have in the original Greek version of St Matthew. It wasn't any sort of joy. It was massive!

St Josemaría used to say that our vocation is like that star. Once you have seen it, keep going, don't give up. There will be times when the clouds won't allow you to see it. But it is still there. It has always been. St Paul says that *"the gifts and the call of God are irrevocable"* (*Ro* 11:29). God doesn't change His mind. If He gave you a vocation and you have seen it, it is real, it is there. So, St Josemaría concluded, you only need to see it once. If you are faithful, once is enough to keep going. And if you don't give up, you can be assured that you will see the star again, maybe a while from now, but you will see it and you will also *"rejoice exceedingly with great joy"*.

At the end of their long journey, we read, they "*saw the child with Mary his mother.*" There you always are, Mary, Star of Sea, making it possible for us to find your Son. I ask you, my Mother, that you keep shedding light on my vocation and that you keep me on my feet, always on my way, *forwards*, never giving up; so that even if I can't see my star, I can still see you, Mary, as my Morning Star.

50

Thank You!

> *Rejoice always, pray constantly, give thanks in all circumstances; for this is the will of God in Christ Jesus for you* (1 Thessalonians 5:16-18).

We have already read about Jose Luis Martin Descalzo. Meditating on the life of his priest-uncle gave young Jose Luis the impulse he needed to follow in his uncle's footsteps and eventually he also became a priest. For many years he had to endure painful sessions of dialysis due to a kidney condition. He died from cancer in 1991, at the age of 60. A few days before his death, he published a letter to God that we reproduce here as our last chapter.

*"**Thank You.** This word could sum up this letter to You God, "my love", because that is all that I have to tell You: thank You, thank You. Looking back from the mountaintop of my life, what do I see except the endless peaks of Your love? In my history there is no region which is not illuminated by Your Mercy towards me. There has never been a time when I did not experience Your loving, fatherly Presence caressing my soul.*

Only yesterday I received a card from a friend who had just heard about my health problems. She wrote to me furiously, "A huge load of rage invaded my whole being, and I rebelled against God for allowing people like you to suffer." Poor thing! Her affection prevents her from seeing the truth. While I am no more important than anyone else, my whole life is a testimony to two things: being and faith. I have suffered more than a few times at the hands of people; I have received curses and ingratitude, loneliness and misunderstanding. **However, from You I have received nothing but endless gestures of affection, including my latest illness.**

First You gave me being, the marvel of being human. The joy of experiencing the beauty of the world. The joy of being part of the human family. The joy of knowing that, in the end, if I put everything in a balance the cuts and bruises will always be far less than the tremendous love which these same people have put on the other side of the balance in my life. Have I been more fortunate than others? Probably. Now, how could I pretend to be a martyr of humanity knowing for certain that I have had more help and understanding than difficulties?

Furthermore, You accompanied the gift of being with the gift of faith. In my childhood I felt Your presence at all times. You seemed very gentle to me. **Your Name never frightened me.** *You planted a fabulous capacity in my soul: the capacity to know that I am loved, to feel that I am loved, to experience Your presence daily in the passing of each hour. There are some people, I know, who curse the day of their birth, who scream at You that they did not ask to be born. I did not request it either, because I did not exist prior to that. But knowing what my life has been, I would have implored You, begging for this same one which You have given me.*

I suppose that it was absolutely necessary to be born into the family You chose for me. Today I would give everything I possess just to have the parents and siblings which I had. All of them were living witnesses to the presence of Your love. Through them I learned so easily who You are. Thanks to them, loving You and loving others became so much easier. It would have been absurd not to love You. It would have been difficult to live in bitterness. Happiness, faith and trust were like the custard which my mother served after supper without fail. If it wasn't served, it was simply because eggs weren't available that day, not because love was lacking. I also learned that pain was part of the game - not a curse but part of the price of living, something which would never be enough to take away our joy.

Thanks to all this (I feel ashamed to say it) pain does not hurt me now, nor does bitterness make me bitter. Not because I am brave but simply because ever since my childhood I have learned to contemplate the positive aspects of life and to take the dark aspects in my stride. It turns out that when they come they're not so dark but just a little grey...

Sometimes I think that I have had "too much good luck". The saints offered You great things. I have never had anything important to offer You. I fear that, at the hour of my death, I am going to have the same thought that my mother had when she passed away: the thought of dying with empty hands because nothing You sent me was unbearable. Not even the loneliness or the desolation which You give to those who are truly Yours. **I'm sorry, but what do I do if You have never abandoned me?** Sometimes I am ashamed thinking that I will die without having been at Your side in the Garden of Olives, without having had my agony in Gethsemane. It's just that You, I don't know why, never took me away from Palm Sunday. Sometimes, in my heroic dreams, I have even thought that I would have liked to have a crisis of faith in order to prove myself to You. They say that authentic faith is proved in the crucible. I have never encountered any crucible other than Your caressing hands.

It's not that I have been better than others. Sin lurks within me. You and I both know how deeply. The truth is, even in the worst times I have not fully experienced the black shadow of evil thanks to Your constant light. Even in misery I have still been Yours. In fact, Your love for me seemed to increase the more mistakes I made.

I also took You for granted during times of persecution and difficulty. You know that even in human things there were always more good people at my side than traitors. For every incomprehension or betrayal I received ten smiles. I had the good fortune that evil never did me harm. Most importantly it never made me bitter inside. Even bad experiences increased my desire to become better and resulted in unexpected friendships.

Later You gave me my astonishing vocation. To be a priest is impossible, You know that. But it is also marvellous, I know that. Today I certainly don't have the enthusiasm of young love as in the first days. But fortunately, the Mass has never become a mere routine, and I still tremble during every confession. I still know the unsurpassable joy of being able to help people and the joy of being able to proclaim Your name to them. You know, I still weep reading the parable of the prodigal son. **Thanks to You, I am still moved every time I recite that portion of the Creed which speaks of Your Passion and Death.**

Naturally, the greatest of Your gifts was Your Son, Jesus. Even if I had been the most miserable person, if misery had pursued me in every aspect of my life, I know that I would only have had to remember Jesus to overcome them. Knowing that You have been one of us reconciles me with all of our failures and emptiness. How is it possible to be sad, knowing that You have walked upon this planet? How could I desire more tenderness than meditating on the face of Mary?

I have certainly been happy. How could I not be? I have been happy here, even outside the glory of Heaven. Look, You know that I am not afraid of death, but I'm not in a hurry to get there either. Will I be able to be any closer to You there than I am now? This is the marvel: we have Heaven from the moment that we are able to love You. My friend Cabodevilla was onto something when he said, "We are going to die without knowing which is the greatest of Your gifts, that You love us or that You allow us to love You."

For this reason it pains me greatly to know people who do not value their lives. Indeed, we are doing something infinitely greater than our own nature, loving You, collaborating with You in the construction of a great edifice of love!

It is difficult for me to say that we give You glory here. That's too much! I am content believing that resting my head in Your hands gives You the opportunity to love me. It makes me laugh a little that You are going to give us Heaven as a reward. A reward for what? You are clever. **You give us Heaven and give us the impression that we deserved it.** *You know very well that love can only be repaid with love. Happiness is not the consequence or the fruit of love. Love is, in itself alone, happiness. Knowing that You are my Father is Heaven. Of course You don't have to give me anything, loving You is itself a gift. You can't give me more.*

In light of all this, my God, I have wanted to talk with You and about You in my final page of my "Reasons for Love". **You are the ultimate and the only reason for my love.** *I have no others. How could I have any hope without You? What would my joy be founded on if I lacked You? What tasteless wine would my love become if it were not a reflection of Your love? You give strength and life to everything. I know very well that my only task as a person is to repeat and repeat Your Name. With that, I take my leave.*

Mary, Mother of Good Counsel, I place myself under your protection. I consecrate myself to the service of Our Lord just as you did, counting on your intercession to be faithful to my calling and courageous in difficulties; to be generous in its demands and to persevere with patience; to be able to say, every day of my life as a good child of yours, my Mother, "*Be it done unto me according to thy word.*"

Do you know iPray with the Gospel?

Taking the Gospel of the day, the *iPray* provides a commentary that can be a trigger for an authentic and personal conversation with Jesus. That time of prayer spent with Jesus is like a 'cooking pot' in which you blend the Words and scenes of Jesus' life, found in the Gospel, together with your daily life, your worries, your family and friends, all heated up by the fire of the Holy Spirit.

iPray with the Gospel is not a ready-made meal you can just throw in the microwave, as if they were some prayers that you read and that's it. It is more like a personal recipe that only you can cook with the help of the Holy Spirit.

Visit us in our website:

Download the app:

iOS	Android

Printed in Great Britain
by Amazon